How to be Number One

in your own world

HOW *to be* NUMBER ONE

in your own world

MANDI NORWOOD

Editor in Chief, *Cosmopolitan*

Thorsons

Thorsons
An Imprint of HarperCollins*Publishers*
77–85 Fulham Palace Road,
Hammersmith, London W6 8JB

The Thorsons website address is: www.thorsons.com

Published by Thorsons in association with *Cosmopolitan* magazine

1 3 5 7 9 10 8 6 4 2

A catalogue record for this book
is available from the British Library

ISBN 0 7225 3958 4

Printed and bound in Great Britain by
Caledonian International Book Manufacturing Ltd, Glasgow

This book is dedicated to:

- My mother for making me believe in myself. Her constant encouragement provided the inspiration for this book.
- My husband, Martin, for his love, patience and fabulous back rubs.
- My two daughters, Rosie and Daisy, who are already showing true signs of being number one in their own worlds.
- All the wonderful *Cosmopolitan* team and Emma Dally, for their support.
- Every single *Cosmopolitan* reader.
- All the amazing people who enlightened me with their inspiring experiences of being number one in their own worlds.
- Rachel Cottam for her thorough research.

Contents

CHAPTER 1

Why You Need This Book

I am not going to pretend I'm a great philosopher. Neither am I going to pretend to be an expert in psychology. This book comes directly from first-hand experience of dreaming, believing and achieving. It also comes straight from the heart.

How To Be Number One in Your Own World is for anyone who dreams they are capable of being great in their chosen life, believes they deserve better than the life they were born into, but doesn't quite know:

A if those feelings are justified
B how to go about turning those beliefs into practical achievements
C how to keep up those beliefs when the rest of the world appears to be fighting or scorning them.

But this book is also about chasing and achieving happiness. About believing you're entitled to be happy in your life. This doesn't necessarily mean happiness at the expense of other people, but simply happiness that you are living the life you want to live, fulfilling your needs and achieving your potential.

I hope this book will provide you with a boost you can tap into at any time, like an earpiece of recordings of encouragement and inspiration. At times we all need a source of motivation that uplifts us and gives us confidence, particularly when friends and family — or our own internal drive — can't sustain what we need. In these pages you will find words written especially for you that inspire self-belief and courage to go on, and to remind you of your many star qualities. No such book has existed until now, at least not one that isn't written by over-bearing psychologists or in language that isn't cheesy or alienating.

This idea came about through my own experiences of believing and achieving, but also of feeling at times sapped of confidence and willpower. Having spoken to many, many young women over years of being an editor of various women's magazines, I realized the greatest gift you could bestow on anyone was permission to dream and confidence in their own abilities. As one woman I particularly admire, Mary Kay Ash (who fulfilled her dream of a mail-order beauty empire worth millions) said:

I believe that if you had the choice of two gifts for your child, $1 million on one side of the scale and the ability to think positively on the other, the greater gift would be the gift of confidence.

On this basis, I began to keep two diaries for my daughters, Rosie and Daisy. I would scribble in them every so often about the great things they'd done, the clever words or sentences they'd piped up, descriptions of acts of amazing kindness, absolute gorgeousness and sheer brilliance. I would tell them how amazing they were, how much I adored them, how loved they were. In moments of shaky self-doubt as they grew up, they could refer to them and at least feel cheered, and at best re-motivated to conquer the world and make their dreams for their own lives come true.

And that's basically what I hope this book will do for you. I have written it for anyone who wants to realize their full potential in whatever capacity that may be – magazine editor, mother, florist, school teacher, rock star, doctor – but who sometimes, if not often, needs an ego prod, a friendly voice to say 'You *can* do it. You can be number one'.

Just Like You

So who am I to write this book? I don't have masses of qualifications (a handful of O levels and two unspectacular A-level passes) and I'm certainly not from a privileged background that gave me a head start. I'm an only child, born in Oldham, about eight miles from Manchester in Lancashire. My parents split when I was seven, which according to statistics, made me a prime candidate for delinquency. My mother remarried when we moved up to the North East, and although I was fairly popular at school, it's fair to say I was pretty revolting as a teenager — spots, gappy teeth and a tendency to vacillate between embarrassing exhibitionism and excruciating tortured sulks.

However, I was extremely fortunate to have been born with (some would say) aspirations beyond my station which were nourished by an innate sense of self-confidence and independence as well as a mother who was never short on encouragement. Oh, and an almost vicious competitive streak which meant that whether I was practising for ballet exams (at which I was pretty good) or studying for my maths GCE (at which I was extraordinarily bad), I was driven to be number one.

For some reason, which I've never tried to fathom, I had a desperate craving to 'be some*one*'. Psychologists would probably put it down to a variety of crazy reasons: deficiencies of character, birth order, early traumas, whatever. But, frankly, it's irrelevant to me — and to you. The bottom line is, for whatever reason, I had a compulsion to reach my full potential; to stretch the boundaries of what was deemed possible for someone like me.

In those confused teenage years, I didn't have a clear vision of my future. Back then, I remember my notion of reaching my full potential involved images of driving a black sports car (I was partial to Ferraris) past a screaming crowd of adolescent male autograph hunters to my mansion in the hills where I would spend my life counting the piles of cash accrued from Oscar-winning performances in Hollywood or sell-out gigs at Wembley.

Fortunately, a certain amount of realism prevailed (despite growing up in the punk years, I had sufficient nous to realize that my singing voice was never going to bring me real glory), and I decided to explore opportunities which involved stretching my two greatest skills: writing entertaining prose and being bloody cheeky.

Having scraped a couple of A-level passes, I accepted my place at journalism college in Darlington. After a few months of trudging through lectures in public administration, law, shorthand and basic journalism, I made my big decision: to be the editor of a glossy magazine. Stuff all that working my way up through the ranks of local papers and, maybe, one day, I'd be a fairly good hack. Hell, there was something bigger out there and I should, at the very least, have a go. What was wrong with attempting to attain it? Someone had to be the editor of these glossy magazines, piles and piles of which cluttered my little yellow and brown floral bedroom (listen, it was fashionable then). And why shouldn't that someone be *me*?

Where was the rule book which stated spotty teenagers couldn't be editors of glamorous magazines? Okay, so I didn't *know* of any spotty teenagers who *had* (my only contact with any kind of glamour was my drama teacher who was the niece of actress Judi Dench), but should I take this to mean it wasn't *possible*? If I didn't try, I wouldn't know for sure. What I did know with any certainty was that I would be a pain in the neck to all those around me, but most importantly to myself, if I didn't pursue that dream.

I won't bore you right now with the minutiae of how I pursued that dream, except to say there were tons of agonizing disappointments along the way (I'll let you into some later). But the constant was the belief in myself and that I had a right to achieve that dream. And I did at a relatively young age. Of course, that dream isn't everybody's bag of biscuits, but that doesn't mean my dream wasn't valid (and this is one of the main lessons of the book!). This is why I feel more than equipped to write about achieving personal dreams, regardless of whether people view your dreams as insignificant, silly or downright impossible; regardless also of your class, looks, education or accent.

The Dream Realized

My personal dream was to be the editor of *Cosmopolitan*. The number one job on the British version of the number one magazine in the world for young women. And, thankfully, it is everything I ever dreamed it would be – exciting, creative, empowering, fun, high-profile, demanding. With that, it's also stressful, competitive, exhausting, of course it is. But fabulous, fun and fascinating? Yes. And my own vision of happiness? Yes, yes, yes.

What I most love about *Cosmopolitan* is that its ethos mirrors my own personal philosophy on life: be the very best you can be, whoever you are. As well as being glamorous and outrageous and sexy and stylish, *Cosmopolitan* is a unique vehicle for writers to be candid with you, their audience, and speak through their articles in a way they'd never dare vocalize. But more importantly, it is regarded by you, our readers, as a best friend, mentor and confidante.

When readers confide in *Cosmopolitan*, they do so about a whole array of topics, from controlling boyfriends and husbands to their collision with colleagues and management at work. But what has struck me over the years as Editor is that what underpins most of your letters is an enormous lack of self-esteem which prevents you from pursuing what you believe is right for *you*. Your dream. It's the single biggest affliction we encounter in our readers — and as we have over two million readers between the ages of 16 and 40, you can bet it's a good cross-section of the female population. This lack of self-esteem compromises our relationships, our career, our sex life, our social life and our potential to have fun, fulfilment and, if we want it, power. It keeps us in relationships that can destroy us, jobs that bore us senseless and social circles that inhibit us. In short, it prevents us from leading the life we want to lead, the life we dream of.

It's true. Despite great new opportunities for women today in every sphere, most still believe they're not only not worthy of success, but not worthy of dreaming in the first place. Crazy! Dreaming, having ambitions, wanting to achieve something great, be someone special, is somehow for many regarded as an indulgence. They don't feel entitled to have aspirations because, for some reason, they don't feel they have a right to grow, move up, up, up ... and possibly away from their social background or the friends they grew up with, or their parents.

I blame it partly on a misplaced loyalty, especially among women. They still feel they must place other people's desires (and other people's desires for them) above their own, even at the risk of frustrations later in life, unhappiness, and worse, regrets. I also blame an inverted snobbery that still exists in many communities that keeps the population in their place, socially and aspirationally. Coming from a fairly tight community, I experienced this kind of inverted snobbery when I dared to move away (only 32 miles, it has to be said) to journalism college. Here's an example, a tiny one admittedly, but symbolic nevertheless ...

Back in the local pub in the town where I grew up, the first night of my college half term, I ordered a gin and tonic. (Hey, it is a free country after all.) But because I hadn't asked for the obligatory lager and blackcurrant, my God, you'd have thought I'd ordered distilled antelope's pee. The dismay! The shock! The anger! 'Oh, too good for us now, are we?' I remember a so-called good friend (at the time) demanded. 'Who the hell do you think you are?' shrieked another.

And you know what? I almost didn't drink that gin and tonic. I almost threw the rather pathetic looking beverage masquerading as a G & T at the nearest rubber plant.

I *almost* gave in to the pressure to have what they were having, to conform to their desires and what they desired and expected of me. Why? You know why. Because it would have been simpler. It would have been nicer. It would have made them feel better about their own drinks and, yes, their own lives. But, hey, it wouldn't have made *me* happy.

In fact, drinking that G & T didn't make me exactly ecstatic either at the time. With every sip, I almost choked on the rejection and disappointment from my peers. But it was a tiny lesson for the future: that in moving on and getting what you want (rather than having what others want for you) you have to be prepared to stand your ground and be persistent, even at the risk of upsetting others by making them question their own choices.

I'm sure you have already been in similar situations of varying magnitude. You probably smack your face up against them every day of your life. You can probably even remember incidents from way back when what you wanted for your future was questioned or laughed at or scorned or dismissed. Cast your mind back to those dreams you had as a child when you wanted to be a ballerina or a vet or an actress or an astronaut. I'm sure you remember the response of those around you. Yes? And I bet it was hardly positive or encouraging. Hmmm. I remember those reactions, too. I remember the maths teacher who scoffed and told me I'd never be a lawyer during my want-to-be-a-lawyer phase because, well, very few women make it as lawyers. Oh, and the well-meaning relatives who laughed at my impertinence when I insisted I'd be a great actress. Yes, I *know* you've been there too, and experienced that kind of put-down. Everyone has.

As editor of *Cosmopolitan*, I have the great privilege of being on the judging panel of The *Cosmopolitan* Achievement Awards. It's a thrilling and fantastically rewarding and inspirational experience, especially when you encounter women such as June Morris who wrote in her entry for the 1998 award:

When I was at school, a career counsellor recommended a career either in modelling or nursing. Working-class, Afro-Caribbean girls were not expected to go to university. I took his advice and qualified first as a nurse, then as a midwife. By any standard I had achieved a lot. But university was still my dream. I knew I had so much more to contribute. It took so much courage to leave a steady career, more so because I had to support myself financially during my studies.

With the same determination and drive, June set about entering the legal profession. Against stiff competition she won the Lincoln's Inn Hardwick Scholarship and today she is an up-and-coming barrister in one of the country's leading chambers.

Imagine, however, if June Morris had succumbed to the expectations others (from the narrow-minded career counsellor to society at large) had of her. Not only would we have been deprived of a brilliant lawyer, but we would also have had one very unhappy, demoralized, frustrated, regretful nurse or model to contend with. Thankfully, she didn't cave in. Thankfully, for her and all the people (us) she represents in court every day of her life, she became number one in her own world. But why did she have to fight so hard to follow her heart?

But this book isn't about whingeing about how things are. It's about making what could be *happen*. It's about acknowledging the situation (society, tradition, human nature) and making it regardless, whatever *it* is.

> *A grapefruit is a lemon that had a chance and took advantage of it.*
>
> **Oscar Wilde**

Permission to Dream

When readers of *Cosmopolitan* write to me at the magazine, I know they're not really asking for solutions to whatever problem they may be experiencing, whether the problem is a controlling partner, manipulative boss, suffocating mother, overpowering friend. What they're really asking for is *permission*. Permission to demand what they really want. Permission to be what they really want to be. Permission to dream.

They're seeking encouragement to believe there is something better elsewhere. They're seeking encouragement to go after their dreams, whatever those dreams may be. But dreams, nevertheless, where they are respected, loved – adored even – fulfilled and *happy*.

They write to us at *Cosmo* because they know we'll give them permission and encouragement. We are not going to feel undermined by their success, as maybe their friends or colleagues would. Neither do we have an agenda which will distort our advice to them. Our lives are not entwined with theirs, so we have nothing to lose by being impartial. We can offer them what possibly no one close to them can: unconditional encouragement and support. We can say, without fear of them abandoning us, GO FOR IT! YOU CAN DO IT! And you know what? That's all you really need to hear to squash your fears and insecurities and be what you want to be.

Unfortunately, as a monthly magazine appealing to a wide audience, we can only do that in small, four-weekly chunks. And most of us, so frightened of making fools of ourselves or not fulfilling our expectations, need more encouragement. Encouragement that not only inspires us to formulate dreams, but make plans and then put them into action. And, not forgetting, encouragement to help us pick ourselves up when plans have gone pear-shaped and inspire us to try and try again. And keep *on* trying.

Encouragement to Go on

Yes, it would be great if we could hook ourselves up to an intravenous drip that supplied a steady flow of encouragement and inspiration. Aaaah, imagine what we could achieve? Imagine who we could be? The world would be full of first-class lawyers, brilliant teachers, sensational actresses, fantastic designers … you name it. I see the effect a few well-chosen words of encouragement have on my two young daughters when they're drawing or skipping or washing my back in the bath. (I get a much better back wash when I tell them how great they are at washing my back than when I don't.)

However, back on Planet Reality, no such intravenous drip exists. Which is why I decided to write this book. God knows, I've been in need of a book like this many a time on my road to being editor of *Cosmo*. (Hey, even now what I need is a book like this to help me write this book!) Having dreams and feeling inspired enough to put your foot on that first rung of the ladder is one thing, but maintaining the momentum to keep it there and take the second, third, fourth and fifth step is as much of a test of willpower, motivation and determination.

I have vivid memories of starting out on my career path and moving from Washington New Town down to London with dreams bigger than the great hulking trunk of crockery and clothes I brought with me. I wrote letters to every magazine under the sun, begging, pleading with them to give me a chance. After each rejection, I approached the next one differently. I'd think, perhaps if this time I signed my name Amanda (not that I was christened Amanda, hell no, I was plain old Mandi), I'd be taken more seriously. Maybe if I wrote a letter in rap form (rap music was cool then, believe me), it would stand out from the rest. Once, I even sent a letter in a balloon in the hope it would prove to my prospective employer I was at least worth a chat. And time and again, the rejections would roll in. Not enough experience, not the required skills, not old enough, not young enough, not qualified enough, not this/not that enough.

I'd phone up my distraught mother, wailing, sobbing 'Why won't anyone give me a chance?'. It was true: having the dream is only the beginning. A great beginning, admittedly, but having the courage and resilience to keep on pursuing the dream in the face of setbacks is just as challenging. Let's face it, it's much easier, faced with disappointment and rejection, to admit defeat and take a less challenging life route. At least you can convince yourself that if only *others* had given you the chance you could have been brilliant. I'm sure you have heard as often as I have people say 'Oh, I could have been a painter/florist/racing driver/tennis player if ...'.

And that's the point. Fulfilling your dreams requires self-belief and the conviction that you're amazing (or at the very least as amazing as everyone else), and that is a quality few of us are born with. It's also a quality which, if

How to Be Number One in Your Own World

we are lucky to be born with, is so often battered out of us during our school years and adolescence when we form ideas of who we are and what we're capable of. We may have had big dreams aged nine or ten, but unless we were bright enough to consistently win applause for being top of the class or best in the school, we enter the big wide world all too aware of our shortcomings and vulnerabilities.

So, submerged from the outset with a detailed knowledge of our fallibilities, it's hardly surprising we lack the confidence to recover from a punch and carry on fighting to be number one in our own world. But consider those you admire for their success, both professionally and personally. What do they have in common? Yes, a desire to be number one in their own world. An acute longing for fame, money, recognition, respect, love – certainly. But what they all share is a source of motivation to overcome setbacks and keep on believing they have a *right* to success.

Take one of the greatest female icons of our time: Madonna. In her own world of music and entertainment, she's number one. How did she get there? Certainly not through nepotism – her mother died when she was five and her father was an engineer. She looked good but she wasn't a great beauty. Yes, she had a good voice, but it wasn't remarkable. But what has made Madonna the wealthiest, most successful woman in show business is her drive and need to win at all costs. In an MTV interview she told the reporter, 'I have the same goal I've had since I was a little girl. I want to rule the world'.

What's more, Madonna doesn't just overcome setbacks, she uses them to spur her on towards further success. When she launched her book *Sex* in 1992, *The Times* called it 'the desperate confection of an ageing scandal addict'. And she was voted Worst Actress for 1993 for her role in the film *Body of Evidence*. But did she wallow in her setbacks? Did she give up her lifelong pursuit of power? Are you joking? No doubt she threw her best china at the kitchen wall or tore up her latest lyrics in anger and frustration or upset. But the reality was that Madonna's net worth in her *low* of 1993 was estimated at over 100 million dollars. Now she's thought to be worth double that amount! So much for the folk who criticized and scorned her. It just shows, it can happen to even the best of us.

Staying at Number One

As if allowing yourself to have a dream about being number one in your world wasn't enough of a challenge. And as if maintaining your self-esteem and overcoming setbacks to get to number one wasn't enough of a test of your character. The truth is, when you get to number one (and you can), maintaining that position can be just as difficult – if not more so.

Being the best attracts competition. In my own world, the competitive world of magazines, *Cosmopolitan* is the number one magazine – in other words, it sells more copies every month than any other glossy magazine for young women. So when people ask me what it's like being the editor of this magazine, I tell them it's fantastic, exciting, glamorous, a dream come true. Because, yes, it is all of those things. But it is also extremely demanding and stressful. There are nights when I lie awake until the early hours wondering how on earth I can think up one more idea that will tempt potential readers to buy *Cosmo* rather than any other magazine. How can I keep on motivating all those wonderful people who work with me on the magazine to keep up the excellence that's got us into this position in the first place? How will I fend off rival magazines battling for this number one slot. And, how do I ensure I (just a girl with a dream) keep the number one job on the number one magazine when there are hundreds of great women out there who claim to be able to do what I do as well as, if not better than, I do? Hell, it's bringing me out in a cold sweat just thinking about it.

In the course of writing this book, I have spoken to many, many women and men who often go through this nocturnal torture themselves. It's easy to be consumed by that old cliché: 'When you're number one, there's only one place you can go – down'. But that is only true if you allow yourself to believe it, if you allow yourself to buckle under the demands of your number one slot rather than using it to spur you on.

Staying number one — whether it's being number one at work, at college, in your drama group, in your relationships — requires a fine balance of ego: high ego to convince yourself you're the best (after all, you got here, didn't you?), that no one deserves this success as much as you, to motivate yourself and those around you; and low ego to allow yourself to keep on learning, growing and pushing boundaries.

Just think for a moment about the people we admire for their success in their chosen field. Who springs to mind? Right now, I'm thinking of Richard Branson. You may not like him, but it's difficult not to admire and respect him. When he started Virgin back in the 1970s, he could have made do with the relative success of his mail-order record company and tiny shop over a shoe store in Oxford Street. He could. Instead, he now has a thriving airline, beauty business, bridal chain, fashion label, finance company and railway in total worth millions. He uses his irrepressible ego to believe he is capable of anything — *every*thing — and take unbelievable risks. Yet Branson balances it with a willingness to listen to others, an acknowledgement that he can always improve, and a caring and motivating attitude to those who work with and for him.

Margaret Thatcher, the longest-serving British prime minister of the 20th century, is a classic example of using limited resources to get to the top and stay there for a prolonged period of time. Her ego was her driving force. You may remember when she told a broadcast interviewer back in 1980:

I am not hard, I'm frightfully soft. But I will not be hounded. I will not be driven anywhere against my will ... I am the leader of the pack. What's a leader for but to lead the pack? Of course they are behind me. If they were in front of me, they would be the leaders.

But, ironically, it was also her ego which ten years later proved to be her downfall and deprived her of her number one slot. She refused to listen to her party or the people of the country whom she served. She refused also to accept she could be wrong.

These are extreme examples, I know. Yet, in the spirit of our new way of thinking about our own potential, not unrealistic either. But I know many people don't wish to be Richard Branson or Anita Roddick or Chris Evans or Madonna or Margaret Thatcher or Gwyneth Paltrow or anyone else who in the narrow sense of the word is deemed successful. The truth is, however, whether you're the prime minister or a terrific primary school teacher, a number one entrepreneur or number one wardrobe mistress, the demands and challenges of success are the same, and we'll explore them in more depth later in the book. You only have to acknowledge and understand them and the only way you can go from your number one slot is up, up and up!

Way to Go!

So now you're convinced: it's only your lack of self-belief that stands between you and your dreams. Belief you are worth listening to. Belief you are a good person. Belief you have great, unique qualities. Belief you can do anything. Belief you're worth loving and respecting. Belief you are a star. Belief you can be whatever you want to be, whoever you are. Belief you are entitled to be number one. Belief you can be – and stay – number one in your own world.

Now it's time to put this book by your bed, in your bag, permanently on your reading table. It will help you to make your dreams and beliefs of being number one a reality. But only you can do it. And you know what? You CAN do it.

Life is short and it's up to you to make it sweet.
Sadie Delaney, author who died aged 109!

CHAPTER 2

What is Success?

We are all born in the gutter, but some of us look to the stars.

Oscar Wilde

Success comes in many shapes and forms. You can be successful in your career. You can be successful at college or university. You can be successful in love. You can be successful in bed. You can be successful in financial terms. And, spiritually, you can be successful. You can be successful in your hobby – cooking, dancing, swimming, travelling, writing poetry, music, painting. Successful having children, looking after them, moulding them into happy, healthy, confident human beings. You can be hugely successful as a friend, as a colleague, as a spouse, as a boss, as an assistant, as a sibling, as a mistress, even as an enemy.

You can be a success at whatever you do. Nothing in the world can stop you being successful, being number one in whatever you do, except you. But first, you need to define what it is you want to be successful at. You can be successful in one area of your life or you can be successful in umpteen areas. You can also be successful in no areas of your life. The choice is yours. Only you have the power to make that decision and only you have the power to take that decision further, to put those thoughts into action and make being number one not a dream, but a reality.

Over the years, our definitions of success have certainly changed – for good and bad. Just go back a handful of decades. My own mother – and no doubt many of your mothers too – grew up in the 1940s and '50s when success for a woman was defined as a good husband, a couple of rosy-cheeked children and a fail-safe recipe for Christmas cake. If they were really successful, they might even have had a convenient and respectable part-time job as a secretary or receptionist. Hey, don't titter – ask them. This was how it was then.

In the 1970s, when I was starting secondary school, success was defined as leaving education with a couple of O levels, landing an office job for a couple of years (if you got a job in a bank, so much the better) and then bowing out from the working world to 'settle down' and have a family. Maybe, if you were really successful, you might even 'go abroad' once a year for your summer holiday.

Then – bang! – along came the mid- to late '80s when our definitions of success turned head over heels. Do you remember? I'm sure you do. It wasn't enough to have a car, was it? Nooooo. To be really successful, you had to drive a Porsche. Neither was it enough to have a steady job. Pah! You didn't even dare utter the S word unless you were bringing home bonuses big enough to sustain a third-world country. Own your own home? Oh puhleeez. If you truly wanted to be taken seriously in the land of the successful, nothing sufficed but a city apartment or swish little pied-à-terre for weekdays, a country retreat for weekend parties *and* a holiday home in the south of France. Phew!

And then came along 'the caring, sharing '90s' when success almost became a dirty word along with ambition, determination and – sshhh! – money. Get to the top of the career ladder? What a vulgar thought! No, success was defined as finding a spiritual teacher to guarantee enlightenment and your place in heaven. Earn pots of cash? Outrageous behaviour! Only the depraved were motivated by money. And we didn't dare confess that we were only interested in a loving, monogamous relationship and working hard to ensure the success of our future family. What were we thinking of when we could be saving trees, helping the homeless or rescuing orphans from war-torn countries?

And now, here we are at the start of a whole new millennium. A thrilling age to be alive. A time when every definition of success has been exhausted and turned into a cliché. But, nevertheless, a time when anything goes and everything is possible. The chef who becomes a lottery millionaire and buys his own restaurant – that's regarded as success now. As is the infertile couple who, after a decade of trying for their own child, become the parents of sextuplets. How about the entrepreneur who starts with one tiny idea and suddenly finds herself a household name with a range of beauty products every woman in the world covets? Or the high-flying executive who gives it all up for a cottage in the country and a life of looking after his or her children?

If you consider these to be extreme examples of success definitions in 2000, I'll come more down to earth. I admire, for example, a friend who has given up her nine-to-five job to pursue what she really wants to do, write and paint. That's success. I also admire the success of another friend who is realizing her ambition to take time out to travel and then have children. One of my oldest friends single-mindedly pursues her career to enable her to pay for the house of her dreams, take four holidays abroad every year ('one every season') and drive a drop-dead gorgeous soft-top car. That too is success. A different kind of success, but success nonetheless. As is this: a woman with whom I became firm friends when we both had Saturday jobs in Dorothy Perkins in Newcastle – she's successful because she is realizing her ambition to study for a Masters degree while enjoying her work in London's East End counselling and caring for people with HIV.

To me – and to you if you met them, although you're bound to know similar people – they are all successful. They are all number one in their own world. And it's as simple as this: they are all pursuing their dreams and achieving them. Their dreams may not be my dreams or your dreams. But they are their dreams. And they're valid dreams; dreams that will make them feel valued, fulfilled, happy.

How to Be Number One in Your Own World

You may say they are lucky. But lucky is a word I choose never to use. Why? Because I firmly believe you make your own luck. In very, very few cases does the realization of a dream just happen to land in your lap. (Come on, even the lottery winner has to make the effort to buy the lottery ticket in the first place.) However, you would be right to say they were lucky in one respect – and one respect alone. They were lucky … no, I can't stand it, let's say they deserve to be *congratulated* … for getting through the mind-fog to arrive at their own definition of success. To define what being number one in their own world really is.

> *Success has very little to do with luck. You can be fortunate to have things, but you don't achieve great things through luck, especially in your career. No business offers you a large salary, or a great deal, out of charity. Even if you were introduced to someone who could help you get where you want to be by a friend of a friend, they won't take you on just because of that. Achieving goals and dreams is about hard work and not cutting corners. Only unsuccessful people put success down to luck.*
>
> **Anna Maxted, writer and *Cosmopolitan* contributing editor**

Having it All?

Now, when our opportunities are so vast and varied, understanding what our world should be, never mind what constitutes the number one position in it, can be extremely difficult. Women – and, yes, men too – the world over fought and won the right to live the '70s *Cosmo* dream, 'to have it all', but we have come to realize there's a price to pay for achieving the 'having it all' dream. Having a wonderful relationship/marriage, bringing up healthy, happy children, holding down a high-earning, fast-track job, managing a home, being a wonderful daughter or son, taking fabulous holidays abroad, being a sex goddess in the bedroom, having responsibility and power and so on and so on, has left a number of high-profile victims in its wake.

Why? Because by saying you *should* want or have it all is as bad as saying you should have nothing at all. That phrase carries someone else's expectations of you and how you should live your life. Under this now archaic regime, many, many women (and men) felt they weren't successful if they didn't have the family, the lover, the job, the pay packet, because we had all fought so hard for the right to have it. As a result they became super-stressed, burnt out, clinically depressed. They discovered they weren't, after all, despite the symbols of their so-called success, number one in their world. They were actually only number four, five or six in many different worlds. They felt neither fulfilled nor happy. And the reason is so simple: they were not doing this for themselves because it would make them truly happy, but because society had suddenly come to expect it of them.

Linda Kelsey, editor of *Cosmopolitan* from 1985 to 1988, was a proponent of this 'having it all' maxim. During her editorship, she featured many articles urging women to go for the 'having it all' dream. God knows, she lived the dream herself. Even after she gave birth to her son, she continued to be a star performer at work as well as at home. She went on to relaunch *Cosmopolitan*'s ailing sister title, *She*, and took the magazine's circulation to great new heights. But, in 1995, Linda found that being all things to all people, with little left over for herself, ate away at her energy and her motivation to go on.

First, Linda was prescribed medication. Then:

... the psychiatrist who had been prescribing my medication suggested I check myself into a private hospital. It was both scary and a relief. I had entered a world in which there were no expectations and no demands ... Slowly, slowly I was beginning to heal.

Don't be mistaken. Linda's experience is not a tale of woe. It has a happy ending in that, these days, Linda has a crystal clear understanding of what being number one in her own world means. She knows what will make her happy. She now works freelance and is able to combine her creative needs with her family and personal needs. But, she concludes:

Doing it all is not the answer for the future. But neither is turning back the clock. Today's woman is a feisty, ambitious, fun-loving girl. But if she wants to avoid the downside of what happened to me, she should think seriously about whether having quite a bit might ultimately be better than having it all.

What Does Success Mean to You?

Let me kick this off by looking at someone like, say, Michael Jackson. If we're talking in bald and basic terms of financial success, then yes, he's made it. Now worth millions, he is undoubtedly successful. However, it doesn't take a brain surgeon to work out that he is most definitely not number one in his world. Why? Simple. He has lived his life trying to be someone else. His domineering father pushed him and his brothers into the show-biz limelight. He didn't ask the young Michael whether he wanted a high-profile career in music. He wrongly assumed that because he wanted it, his sons must want it too.

Michael pursued the dream of his father – to be number one in his father's interpretation of the world. Now nearing middle-age with numerous best-selling albums and world tours under his belt, although outwardly successful, he seems far from being contented or happy. He has attempted through years of reconstructive surgery and ill-fated relationships to find contentment within himself. To *be* himself. To discover what will truly make him happy. But has he found it? Is he number one in his own world? No. He is – or was – number one at one time in the world of music, in his father's world, but never in his own.

It's easy, as outsiders, to see the cruelty of Michael Jackson's experience very clearly indeed. It isn't so easy to see our own. Extricating ourselves from our parents' aspirations for us requires huge strength of character. You hear parents all the time saying 'I only want what's best for him/her'. But 'what's best' invariably translates as 'what I want for him/her and what's best for me'.

No child, however rebellious, really wants to battle with the disappointment or disapproval of their parents. We would far rather see our parents beam with pride and delight. But even today, grown women and men will confess (some of them through letters to me at *Cosmo*) that they only studied to be a teacher/doctor/solicitor/architect because that's what their parents said they should do. Admittedly, they say, at the time they had no idea what they wanted as an alternative. But now, having travelled someone else's road, they find themselves discontented, unfulfilled, stressed and regretful.

Conversely, there are also parents who kill the dreams of their children because they themselves don't have any aspirations for themselves or their offspring. Nothing beats a dream to a pulp more than a parent (someone to whom we instinctively look for reassurance or confirmation of what's right) declaring 'You'll never be a writer, you can't bloody string a sentence together' or 'You? An actress? Don't make me laugh'.

Fortunately for me, my mother was determined to give nothing but encouragement to her own children. 'You want to be a ballerina? Great. Do it.' she said. A single parent, she sacrificed her own interests and managed to scrape together enough money for me to take ballet lessons, not once, but two or three times a week. Finally, at the age of 12, having been rejected by the Royal Ballet School and turned down for a local authority grant to attend Elmhurst Stage School in Surrey, my dream of being a prima ballerina dissolved and I set my sights elsewhere. After that, I dreamed of being everything from a member of the Royal Shakespeare Company to an environmental health officer. I even flirted with the idea of being a policewoman or a chorus girl. But you know what? Never once did my mother poo-poo the idea. Which meant when I finally decided being the editor of a women's magazine was what I really, *really* wanted to do, I always knew I could count on her support. Thanks to her, I had an over-riding belief I could do it. As well as that, she'd believe in me, when many others (and you know who you are!) did not.

Having enjoyed and benefited from this constant source of encouragement, and having also encountered those who did not, I know how vital it is when deciding what being number one in your own world really means. I hope, however, that whatever your experiences have been, this book is already enabling you to see the validity of your dreams and how to make them a reality.

> *I can't imagine anything worse than being a good girl — this is my life and I really don't care what anyone thinks about the choices I make.*
>
> **Cher**

Breaking Free – and Finding What You Want

Even with family support and encouragement, it's difficult to escape peer pressure, that longing everyone experiences to be one of the gang, especially when we're at the stage in our lives (late teens) when we're making crucial decisions for our future.

When you've grown up and gone through school with a group of people, the easiest route is to follow the flock. And this can cloud judgement when you're deciding whether to go on to further education or not, and if you decide you want to, then choosing where and what you want to study. When everyone else you know and admire is choosing to go to Manchester or Exeter for the next three years, how tempting it is to do exactly the same, whether it's what you really want or not. And if they're all enrolling for business studies? Well, why shouldn't you? Especially if you're not entirely sure what you really want to do.

But it doesn't stop there does it? Maybe you're now in your mid-20s or early 30s and close friends are coupling off, getting married. Some maybe even starting families. And then, hell, from not-for-one-second even considering hooking up long-term with someone, you suddenly find yourself racing down the aisle just so you won't be last on the shelf. What's more, only a year ago, the thought of having children was physically repulsive. Now, a couple of your peers have popped one or two out and kerpow! — you feel you have to as well. After all, if you don't, there's a risk you won't be part of the inner circle any more. You won't be accepted at dinner parties or family picnics in the park. You won't belong.

The desire to fit in with our peer group is so strong, we can chug through our lives never once (or hardly ever) asking ourselves what we really want. We can mistakenly believe that because everyone else is doing it, it must be the right thing to do. But only we have to live with our decisions, no one else. If we're fortunate, we'll be content and fulfilled by accident, rather than by design. But the risk is great. It's far safer to take control of the decision-making. Which is why it's never too late to define success in your own world. And never too late to enjoy it.

> *Make voyages. Attempt them. That's all there is.*
>
> **Elaine Dundy**

Escaping Social Pressures

Opportunities and what's regarded as acceptable for women (and men) have certainly increased and improved a zillion-fold since our mothers had to make decisions about their future. Women now grasp opportunities and excel in every field. Nothing is beyond us any longer. So why, you ask, include a section on society's expectations?

Well, for instance, because the world still goes two by two. This means that if you don't want to be part of a couple and would be happier striking out single, society's expectations can make your life, if not miserable, sometimes isolating, embarrassing and, strangely, costly (such as single-room surcharges in hotels). And society still expects every woman to at least want a child, even if she doesn't bear one. A woman who openly declares she doesn't have any desire to be a mother is greeted with, at best, disbelief ('Ooooh, just you wait ...'), at worst, scorn ('She's a hard bitch'). And if you don't slot into this heterosexual world? You can wave goodbye to even the most basic legal rights enjoyed by straight couples.

Need I go on? Okay. Girls are still expected to be the caring, gentle, considerate members of society, while it's acceptable for a man to be impetuous, arrogant, selfish, even violent. Society shudders with horror when it encounters a woman who deserts her family to pursue her career – this is the stuff not just of gossip, but of ranting newspaper articles and sensationalist documentaries. Equally, when a man decides to put his career on the backburner to fully embrace his responsibilities and desires to be a full-time father, society regards him as a curious phenomenon, to be, in turn, marvelled at as well as pitied.

If you want to turn your back on society's expectations, you can, of course, do so. But the consequences can be almost impossible to stomach. *Still*. Even now. Even at the start of a whole new millennium, the force of social stereotypes can be enough to send you hurtling back into a life of conforming where dreams are for keeping to yourself and aspirations are for squashing – *flat*.

But if maintaining the status quo is the simple option, it isn't the most satisfying. In fact, it contradicts the whole ethos of this book. Because if that is the driving force behind the decisions you make, you will never be number one in your own world. How can you be? You haven't positively chosen what that world is. You have allowed others to choose your world for you. Other people – people who don't even know you, let alone care about you – have taken control of your destiny and your potential to feel valued, respected, happy and motivated.

How to Be Number One in Your Own World

> *There are hazards in anything one does, but there are greater hazards in doing nothing.*
>
> **Shirley Williams**

Define Your Own Success

Let's get this straight. When we talk about success in this book, we are really talking about being number one in your own world. And being number one in your world means your happiness, self-respect and fulfilment is central to the theme. So this book isn't about being famous or rich at the expense of happiness. No way. If you're rich but unhappy, you're certainly not number one in your own world, as your unhappiness shows the world of fantastic wealth was never meant to be your world after all. Does that make sense?

Of course, there's a good side and bad side to every decision you make. But once you have made that decision, it's about weighing up the bad against the good. Does the happiness I feel in my situation outweigh the stress or the exhaustion of maintaining it? Do my feelings of fulfilment and contentment override the feelings I sometimes experience of sacrificing other possibilities in my life? If the answer is yes, hurrah! If you answer no, what you perceive to be success is not success at all … it's compromise.

Being number one in your own world boils down to a very simple equation. Happiness = Success. Success = Happiness.

If the equation is so simple – and it is – the first question you must ask yourself, surely, is what will make *me* happy? Is it creative fulfilment? Is it having and bringing up children? Is it decision-making? Is it having a structure in your life? Is it being a free spirit? Is it working within a team? Or is it isolation? Adulation? Is it taking care of a home? Is it being your own boss? Is there a cause you firmly believe in? Is there an environment in which you know you feel your most content and happy? Is power over other people what presses your buttons and makes you feel energized and happy? Or do you get your kicks from helping other people maximize their life? Do you thrive on setting goals and beating targets? Or are you at your happiest with long-term projects?

Only once you have asked yourself a series of questions like this can you define what your own world is. (Being number one in it is your second strategy.) Author, Ruth Rendell, explained:

I've always been a storyteller which I think is more important than actually writing. But I write for pleasure. I write because I like it.

She makes a great point. So if asking yourself questions leaves you stumped, you can also make a list of elements in your life that you know you will like and that will make you happy. Here's a list you could use. Tick those that apply to you:

I AM HAPPY WHEN …

I'm being creative ☐

I'm with children ☐

I'm among people my own age ☐

I'm among older people ☐

I'm among younger people ☐

I'm on my own ☐

I'm working quickly ☐

I have time to think and consider possible outcomes ☐

I have targets ☐

I'm making decisions ☐

I'm part of a small team ☐

I'm part of a big team ☐

I'm leading a team ☐

I set my own goals ☐

I have a structured pattern to my life ☐

I have no one to answer to ☐

I'm being paid regularly ☐

I'm being paid for each job ☐

I'm not earning money ☐

I'm earning a single figure salary ☐

I'm earning a two figure salary ☐

I'm earning a three figure salary ☐

I'm earning a four figure salary ☐

I'm earning a five figure salary □

I'm earning a six figure salary □

I work to bonuses □

I have lots of tasks at the same time □

I can concentrate on one task at a time □

I'm at home □

I'm in an office □

I'm outdoors □

I'm changing people's lives □

I feel I'm working for a global cause □

I'm working with numbers □

I'm warm □

I'm cool □

I can take the spotlight □

I can work behind the scenes □

I'm always meeting new people □

I'm in the city □

I'm in the country □

I'm by the sea □

I'm responsible for other people's happiness □

I'm not responsible for other people's happiness □

I'm surrounded by numbers □

I'm surrounded by words □

I'm surrounded by technology □

I'm surrounded by colour and texture □

I'm with animals □

I'm in a quiet environment □

I'm in a noisy environment □

I'm in an ordered environment ☐
I'm in chaos ☐
I have deadlines ☐
I'm dispensable ☐
I'm indispensable ☐
I'm idolized ☐
I know what's around the corner ☐
I don't know what's around the corner ☐
I need to look smart ☐
I need to be casual ☐
I don't have to care what I look like ☐

> *I worked at Thomson holidays for a while, but there was too much sitting in meetings. What I was really interested in was food and drink. And I was determined to find a job in something I liked. I think that would be good advice. Make your work life as close as possible to something you positively enjoy.*
> **Jancis Robinson**
> **Wine-writer and broadcaster**

If there are elements of your life you know will make you happy which don't appear on this list, feel free to add them. Also – and this is important – feel free to amend your list. After all, what we regard as success and makes us happy at 20 doesn't necessarily make us happy at 30. But the point is, you can use this list throughout your life. Not only when you are defining your world and creating your own meaning of success within it, but also when you need confirmation in the process of being number one in your world that your life is measuring up to what *you* want.

Once you have completed your list, it's time to ask yourself what you're good at. Of course, it doesn't necessarily follow that just because you're good at something, you should confine your world to just that. Pursuing something in which you excel won't necessarily make you number one in your own world (sorry, but cast your mind back to what we discussed earlier about Michael Jackson: he's a genius musician and song-writer, but he isn't happy). But it tends to be the case that if we're good at something, we'll take joy from it. (How much joy, of course, depends on other circumstances, such as parental or peer pressure as we've discussed earlier, or changing events as we'll tackle later.)

Everyone is good at something, even though at times we may convince ourselves – or believe if others tell us – we're not great at anything at all. Okay, so you can't draw for toffee, but you may be a great listener, a terrific cook, amazing with numbers and statistics. You may feel you have the fashion sense of a turnip. Who cares? Chances are you're fabulous with children, or a scrupulous driver, a precise and fluent writer or amazingly quick at learning new languages. I know I am utterly dreadful at sewing. As for understanding figures and accounts? Forget it. Numbers leave me reeling. And because I'm dreadful at maths, I loathe even basic sums. But, hey, if you need a slogan or a way to sell a magazine, I'm your woman. I'm good at it. And do I love what I do? You bet.

How to Be Number One in Your Own World

The most important thing in life is to step back and ask, 'Am I happy?'. Define your own measures of success. Decide what success should feel like for you personally. Define the parameters within which you are going to work — for example, for me, I'm not prepared to work weekends or more than two nights a week unless there is a real disaster. So part of my success criteria is feeling the balance between work and family. Unless you set the pace, you'll get sucked in to whatever is going on out there.

If you're not happy, then you must take steps. I have had to do that in the past. I had a non-communicative boss and I was working away from home. In retrospect, I tried to hang in too long. I should have cut the umbilical cord earlier. Now I'm more aware of when things are not feeling right. I would take action more quickly. In the end, I left that job.

Janette Anderson, first woman Director of Railtrack, Scotland

Don't be Afraid to Create Your Own World

So you've ticked the list — or created your own list — of what makes you happy. For some, it will now help define the world in which they want to be number one. And as we've discussed, defining your world, understanding its components, represents the first rung of the ladder to being number one. But I'm realistic enough to know that some of you may still be confused. After all, each and every one of us possesses personality contradictions. In other words, you may enjoy solitary work, but isolation unnerves you. Or you may dream of being in a fulfilling, respectful relationship but the notion of commitment fills you with dread. You may want to be a wonderful, considerate mother, but the idea of trailing off to Tumble Tots and playing with Playdough turns you into a seething mass of irritation.

Oh, wouldn't it be wonderful if we could slot ourselves into clear categories? If only you could assume that just because you adore music and children and play keyboards as proficiently as Elton John, you would make a wonderful piano teacher and feel content you'd made it, that you were number one in your world. Hmmm, maybe you would if only being a piano teacher also fulfilled your need to be a part of a team, or experience a daily adrenalin rush, or make a million pounds ... or whatever your other desires may be.

For some, slotting themselves into ready-made opportunities is easy. It's what they want. Thankfully, for me, I didn't have to create the job as editor of *Cosmopolitan*. My dream world already existed. And I knew it would offer me what I aspired to: creative fulfilment, an opportunity to work with a team and to help other people (readers of *Cosmo* as well as staff members), a good salary, a car, leadership opportunities and, yes, opportunities to step into the spotlight ... not all the time so that I couldn't step out of my front door without being mobbed (that, for me, would be too much), but just enough to give me a buzz.

But I know many, many people – maybe you're like them – who understand what will make them happy, what their world *could* be like ... if only that world (that job, that relationship, that environment, whatever) existed. Let's face it, if society defines who we are by what we are (i.e. a nurse, the chairman of a company, a novelist, a waitress), it stands to reason that, if what we want to be does not exist, we feel we have no place in society. We feel aimless, depressed, demotivated.

Alicia Pivaro, who is now Director of RIBA Architecture Centre, told me she felt just like this early in her career, until a chance meeting changed her perspective of life for ever:

I remember meeting a man on a train on my way back from Heathrow. He worked for the Prudential and he asked what I did. It was difficult telling people what I did at the time as I didn't really have a job title. So I used to say I did 'bits and bobs'. So I was telling him the sort of things I did, but that I never really knew what I wanted to be or whom I wanted to work for. And his advice was this: if you can't find the job you want to do, go out and make that job or make that company! It's advice I've heeded ever since.

Doesn't that make brilliant sense? I love that advice. Who says you can't create the world in which you want to be number one? Just because it doesn't currently exist doesn't mean it can't or shouldn't. Simply because you can't find happiness and a positive place in society as it is doesn't mean you can't change elements of society to suit you and what you want. There is no rule book that says you have to live like everyone else. Opportunities are for creating as well as taking. Wow! With this in mind, how liberated do you feel? Hell, the possibilities for you – for anyone – are endless!

Everybody is good at something. You may have an eye for colour, or be fabulous with children or making your own clothes. True success is discovering what you're good at. I had seventeen secretarial jobs before I finally left to give editing and copywriting a chance. And that's when I finally found something I could excel in.

Helen Gurley Brown, founder of *Cosmopolitan*

CHAPTER 3

Defining Number One

So what exactly do I mean by being number one? Is it being at the very top of your tree, the biggest boss of the biggest company? The one who receives all the applause for being star of the show? The one who wins the race, makes the most money, achieves the highest targets?

No. Being number one is dead simple. It means being YOU. It means having a thorough understanding of what makes you buzz with vitality, puts a grin on your face, gives a point to your life, makes you glad to be YOU, living YOUR life. It means throwing off everyone else's expectations of you and drilling right down to the core of who you are and what makes you tick.

It means having a no-holds-barred idea of what you're capable of and what your potential could be. Not being restricted by what's gone before — where you were born, the values you grew up with, the cruel experiences of your past.

Number one is not the person everyone thinks they know. It's the person you know. When others — your parents, your spouse, your best friend or boss — say between pursed lips, 'Oh, I *know* you ...', they are not saying, 'I *really* know you …' but putting up boundaries and obstacles. They are defining you by what they have seen in the past, not what they may see of you in the future.

Whenever someone says 'I know you …' (and, believe me, they say it often), it is invariably followed by a negative. 'I know you … you'll get half-way through and get bored/chicken out/say you want X but really mean Y …' You know the sort of thing. It's a form of control. It's a form of stopping you in your tracks, of making you fearful by forcing you to face up to potential obstacles. The phrase 'I know you …' may be said with good intentions, but it is rarely accurate and productive. Instead of saying 'I know you …', what they're really saying is, 'You can't …'.

Being number one is all about saying I know who I am and I *can* …

Looking After Number One

I feel sorry for this saying. These four little words have become so synonymous with selfish, cruel behaviour that we daren't countenance its application to our own lives. But, for crying out loud, if you don't look after number one, no one else will. It doesn't mean you can't look after number two, three, four and five as well (personally, I give you much more credit). You can look after number one and still be a good, decent, kind, sensitive person, but

How to Be Number One in Your Own World

looking after number one means not forgetting that you have needs and dreams that must be recognized and acted upon if you are to be a whole, happy person.

Looking after number one means allowing yourself to be happy, making your happiness and wellbeing a priority in your life. It means taking control of your destiny and the way you want to live your life, rather than off-loading the responsibility onto someone else. Looking after number one is about recognizing that if you *don't* look after number one, you can't look after numbers two, three, four and five as effectively.

Number one is the most important person in your life. It's what propels you out of bed and gives you the energy to do what you have to do, whether these activities are self-indulgent or beneficial to a group of other people. Number one may not be the only motivator, but it is certainly the only doer. And doing anything, from breezing through an interview to climbing Everest, can only be done by *you*.

Many people say you can't control your own destiny, but if you can't, who can? You know that you alone can't make someone else happy, long-term, day in day out. They have to do things that make them happy, they have to take control of their own happiness. It isn't fair to push that responsibility onto you, is it? Of course not. So if that's the case, you must apply the same logic to yourself. Only you can make yourself truly happy and fulfilled and that requires looking after number one.

Let me make it simpler. You know you are looking after number one when:

- You can honestly say you're happy.
- You will be able to look back at what's happening right now and say, it wasn't necessarily easy, but it was good.
- You smile more than you frown.
- Any regrets you have are as a consequence of your own decisions, not decisions of others.
- You're at your happiest when you're doing your life, rather than dreaming about your life.
- You can look forward with as much glee as you look back.

Being number one is about deciding what will make *your* life – and all its components – the very best it can possibly be. And doing it.

> *From early on, I have felt you have to take responsibility for yourself. I was the eldest child and family life was not always easy. You have to create your own opportunities, make your own luck. If you're not going to do it, nobody else will.*
>
> **Amanda Levete, Architect and Partner of**
> **Future Systems**

Believing in the Power of One

It only takes one person to make a cup of tea, bake a cake, write a letter, have an idea, plant a tree, drive a car, throw a javelin, swim the Channel, scale a mountain, discover penicillin, change a nation's policy, start a discussion, end a war.

If it only takes one to achieve any or all of these tasks, it's crazy to underestimate the power of one. One person has the ability to achieve all of the above – or at least the majority of the above. You are that one person. There is only you as far as your potential to achieve is concerned.

But here's the rub. One person also has the power to break a cup, burn a cake, bin a letter, ignore an idea, dig up a tree, crash a car, break a javelin, not take the leap into the Channel, give up the pursuit of a cure-all, sit on the fence of change, refuse to discuss, and start a war.

One person is mightier than any force of nature and certainly mightier than fate. Trusting in luck or someone else will not get you anywhere. You have so much power to make the life you want possible, it should almost be a criminal offence for anyone to ignore or deny it!

Think about your own life to date. Some of the things you take for granted will actually be huge achievements. Hey, standing and walking on two feet, for starters … yes, I know it's basic, but you did it. Okay, zoom forward to right now … Do you have a job? Can you speak Italian? Can you make people laugh? Have you given birth? Did you pass your driving test? Make Christmas lunch for two, four, six?

All of these are achievements. Whether you think of them as great achievements or insignificant events is up to you. The truth is you achieved them, didn't you? No one can take that away from you. Okay, you may have been helped along the way (or, in the case of childbirth, you may have needed a second person to contribute to the result!) but it was YOU who made it happen. Think about it for a second ...

If you can do all these things, why can't you do more? There is no answer to that question because you *can* do more. You can do anything you like. Which means you can either go for it, or you can listen to the little voice inside which says you can't or shouldn't. If you don't go for it, it's only you stopping it happen. It's you who is giving in to your fears or doubts – or the fears and doubts of other people.

Can you believe this? Even in the middle of writing this book, I fell into exactly the same trap. A very good friend of my husband's came to dinner. We were discussing what we were going to do with the squalor masquerading as our garden. Ray told us how when he'd moved into his house, his garden was far, far worse than our messy patch of lawn, yet he'd landscaped the lot, built a terrace, erected a summer house, and planted a rose garden to put the Chelsea Flower Show to shame. I was filled with admiration, and as I gasped in awe when he produced the photographs to prove it, I found myself sighing 'Oh, I could never do that!'

'Course you could,' retorted Ray. 'No, I'm sorry,' I said, 'I just have to look at a blade of grass and it wilts.' 'Me, too,' Ray replied. 'But I just thought, if those idiots on TV can do it, then I can too. So I bought a book and some tools and got on with it.'

The next day, I felt thoroughly pathetic. Here I am writing a book about how anything is possible, how you can do whatever you want to do and yet giving up on my garden (the garden, it has to be said, I dreamed about for years) without even trying. Suffice to say, I now have a book (okay, four books and a stack of gardening magazines), some tools and a table full of brochures for summer houses. No, I haven't made a start on it … yet. But I will. I will. Anything is possible.

But it just goes to show how quickly I, you, we deny our potential almost unconsciously. What on earth was I afraid of? What's the worst that could happen if I *did* attempt to turn my little garden into the grounds of Hampton Court? My hands might get covered in blisters, I might dig up a few plants thinking they were weeds and the summerhouse might resemble something that Jack built. But would it kill me? No. Would everyone laugh? Maybe. (Actually, knowing my friends, they'd split their sides, but hey …) However, the best that could happen is that I'd have loads of fun giving it a go and a garden that not only looked great (or a damn sight better than it looks right now) but was all my own work. Something of which I could be extremely proud, that gave me a huge sense of achievement, fulfilment and happiness whenever I looked at it. What's more, I would have fulfilled a dream ... and surely that's the ultimate.

My first real success was an exhibition I set up in 1994 called 'Tasty: Good enough to eat' when I'd just come back from LA and some of that American optimism had rubbed off on me. My partner said 'Just do it.' So I got sponsorship and I did it – all by myself – and it was a great success. It made me realize the sort of cultural impact one person can make.

Alicia Pivaro, Director of RIBA Architecture Centre

As a maths teacher in the 1970s, if you were interested and committed, it was easy to rise through the stages to become deputy head. But when I got there, I decided I wanted to be a head. I looked at people who were heads and I thought they were such a dull bunch. They were nearly all men – especially in mixed schools – just scores of grey-suited men and they were so boring. There were very few women heads, but I just looked at these men and thought 'My God, if they can do that, I can.' And I did. Since then, if I've ever needed encouragement I just say to myself, 'Come on, Katherine, you can do it.'

Kathy Heaps, Principal of John Kelly Girls Technology Centre, London

How to Be Number One in Your Own World

It's up to you. There is nothing you can't do. Underestimate the power of one – your power – and you deny your potential and the happiness, achievements and fulfilment you deserve.

> *You should never underestimate your power to make things happen and to do things for yourself.*
> **Anita Roddick, founder of the Body Shop**

Being Number One

When I started writing this book, I talked long and hard with people I admired and who fascinated me, and people from whom I and you could learn. In the process, alternative dimensions to my own personal theory were kicked up for discussion. But if my beliefs were challenged, they were invariably validated by the end of our chat. I remember one such 'chat' with a great friend and colleague, Duncan Edwards, who is now Deputy Managing Director at the National Magazine Company and with whom I spent four years working alongside as Editor and Publisher on *Company* magazine. Curious to hear his thoughts on being number one in your own world, I told him about this book. After all, as someone I've respected for years for his single-minded determination and shrewd business sense, I was bound to pick up a nugget of information I could pass on to you.

Instead, over lunch, Duncan listened me out and then asked a typically insightful question: 'Doesn't being number one in your own world mean that by necessity everyone else – including those you love – must be forced into second or third place or lower in your world?' No one had asked me that before or since, but it's a point that needs addressing right here and now.

The short answer is no. Not at all. Of course not.

The long answer, if you're ready, is this: Being number one in your own world is not about riding roughshod over everyone by letting them do the work so that you can take the glory or profit. It isn't about stampeding over other people's feelings for the sake of your own. Nor is it about being utterly selfish in pursuit of your own happiness, grabbing as you go all the good things life has to offer and leaving behind a trail of destruction and misery.

No, truly being number one in your own world is about being the very best you can be. It's about pursuing all your dreams at once and wanting the very best for you and those you care about, however far and wide the reach of what and who you care about extends. Being number one in your world is about recognizing that your happiness and fulfilment is as important as anyone else's and that you were put on this earth not only to do good to others, but to be good to yourself. Being number one in your own world is about exploiting your own potential, living life 100 per cent. It isn't about excluding others from your dreams and enjoyment, but involving them and allowing them to benefit from your achievements and the happy highs that inevitably result. It's about maximizing your time alive and everything you are. It's about saying yes to opportunities and excelling in them.

A colleague who has become a friend, Jenny Swift (who is also a director for a leading PR agency), says 'I'd define being number one in your own world as feeling what you're achieving is absolutely right for you – whatever that may be – and making no apologies for it.' Damn right. 'But,' she's also quick to point out, 'it takes effort. Being number one in your own world isn't necessarily about taking the easy option. It's about striving to reach your full potential in whatever you're doing.'

So, being a number one mother isn't about popping out children and letting them fend for themselves while you sit back and eat chocolates and watch TV. Being a number one mother is about ploughing all your energies into motherhood and being as brilliant as you can be – cuddling, nurturing, encouraging, inspiring, disciplining and rewarding. It's about instilling the best values in your children, supporting them and their school, getting to know other parents to inspire you and provide other dimensions for your children's free time. It's about being active and proactive, knowing that what you put into your role as mother is equal to what you'll get out of it, now and in the future. For your children, yes, but as important, for you. Being a number one parent is not just about getting up in the morning and performing necessary functions, but performing everything you do in your role as a parent as best as you possibly can – or even better than you may have thought possible.

Being a number one colleague isn't just about minding your own business, getting on with the job and reaching targets set by your boss. It's also about learning, inspiring others, embracing ideas, being committed and loyal, giving more than is basically required, self-motivating and pushing yourself beyond boundaries, working harder and being worth more than the money you're paid. Being number one at work isn't even about being the highest paid or number one in the hierarchy of your office or ward or shop – it's about knowing you're being the very best you can be at what you're doing. And that what you're doing feels right for you, as well as your organization.

Being a number one spouse or partner isn't just about paying half the bills and providing company when required. Neither is it about being worshipped and calling all the shots in your relationship. It's about being sensitive to your partner's needs and feeling empowered to discuss your own. It's also about treating the relationship as a prized possession (not taking it for granted), and having the confidence to allow it to blossom in surprising directions. It's about having the self-esteem to support your partner's dreams, while never losing sight of your own. It's about ploughing into the relationship as much as you expect in return. Are you a number one spouse or partner? Maybe it's time to ask yourself 'Would I go out with/be married to me?'

Being number one in your own world is about choosing the world in which you want to exist and then being number one in it. It isn't about other people's ideology, only your own. A colleague I admire for her clear and optimistic view on life is *Cosmo*'s Executive Creative Editor, Leah Hardy. I love her definition of being number one in your own world which is:

Imagine you're at a party and you overhear someone describe you and your life to another party guest. If you disagree with or don't recognize the person being described, take action. If you like what you hear and feel proud of the description, you're number one in your own world.

I wanted to be the best. I never wanted to be rich. I just wanted to be the best at whatever it was I was doing.
Rose Johnson, Chief Inspector of Schools,
London Borough of Brent

If you do the best you can, you can't fail in your dreams.
Helen Gurley Brown, founder of *Cosmopolitan*

You're not number one if …	You are number one when …
You live by rules.	You live by your own rules.
You strive to reach imposed standards.	You set your own standards.
Trophies and trimmings are the symbols of success.	Exhilaration and pride in what you have achieved are your success benchmarks.
You're preoccupied with where you came from.	You focus on where you're heading.
You look to achieving within other people's boundaries.	You believe the only boundaries are in your imagination.
You fulfil others' expectations.	You fulfil your dreams.
You look for reasons.	You exploit possibilities.
You believe in the greater good.	You believe in the power of one.
You make excuses for who you are.	You delight in your uniqueness.

CHAPTER 4

The New Sense of Self

There has never been a better time to aspire to be number one in your own world – and to achieve it. Following a century in which every decade can be summed up by unique social experiences which have impacted on our individual behaviour and our attitudes to ourselves, we have emerged into this millennium with a new, stronger, more valid sense of who we are and our role in the world. In short, a new sense of self.

If we haven't learned anything from our experiences of the last century, we have at least learned this: what you are lies in who you are. Your power lies not in causes, material possessions or acquired spirituality, but you. Only you have responsibility for setting your own value and, in so doing, your value in society. Great things do not arise from how society governs the individual, but how the individual governs society. The new sense of self is about taking what's right for you from society and then benefiting society by giving back what you can, by being aware and confident of what and who you are and acknowledging there's no limit to what you can do.

The new sense of self is about having the confidence to be happy and content in your own life, knowing that the happiness and contentment of those around is more likely to occur because of it. And it's having the self-awareness to march to your own internal beat rather than marching to someone else's. It's about listening to your intuition and following it rather than reacting to someone else's responses. The new sense of self is about being self-centred; not self-obsessed, not selfish but, yes, self-centred. Not only understanding what makes you tick and sets the very core of you alight, but acknowledging the need to respond to it because the outcome will be positive for you and those who care for you.

The new sense of self is not about being great within a set of predetermined boundaries, but about individuals setting their own boundaries ... and, in many cases, crashing through them. It isn't about meeting expectations, but celebrating your own achievements. Identifying a clear role for yourself and a quotient of happiness you deserve within the universe and knowing, believing that you as an individual with all your strengths and weaknesses, foibles and fallibilities can achieve a sense of satisfaction and purpose. It's about not being afraid of your individuality, but relishing it. It's about being unique. Now the millennium has arrived, it's time to truly celebrate you. Your you-niqueness.

Old sense of self	New sense of self
Being satisfied.	Being happy.
Feeling exploited.	Exploiting your value.
Being self-obsessed.	Having self-esteem.
Meeting expectations.	Setting your own goals.
Trusting to destiny.	Following your own intuition.
Being a good citizen.	Identifying your own role within society.

> *For the first time ever, it's okay to acknowledge you value yourself highly. It's okay to want the very best for yourself. It isn't arrogance, it's a commendable quality. If you had admitted to putting yourself first in the past, others would have regarded you as selfish and unfeeling. But society has now realized the better you are for yourself, the better you are as a member of society. The more fulfilled you are as an individual in terms of having and achieving personal goals and successes, the better you'll be in a group.*
>
> **Sarah Kennedy, Commissioning Editor,**
> *Cosmopolitan*

Celebrate Your You-niqueness

No, you're not perfect. But you know what? That's a good thing. You're better than perfect. You're *unique*. And all your little obsessions and compulsions are precisely what makes you you. But before you can appreciate your sense of self and work on being number one in your own world, it's worth appraising your individuality, your *you-niqueness*.

Ask Yourself This: Who are You?

Take this quick quiz to discover a theme to your individuality (guaranteed, no one else will give the same answers).

A If your life philosophy could be summed up as a T-shirt slogan, what would it be?

B Do you have a nickname? What do you think it should it be?

C What would be the title of your memoirs?

D If you overheard someone describing you to a party guest, what would they say? What would you want them to say?

E If people used your name as a verb (as in 'She did a real Mandi' or 'She really Julied it last night') what would they be talking about?

F You'll eventually become famous for what?

G Which actress deserves to play you in the film of your life?

H Which three qualities do you most admire about yourself?

I Which song sums you up best?

Good fun, wasn't it? When was the last time you allowed yourself to take centre stage like this? Most of us spend so much time trying to figure out how we can please, comfort and delight everyone else on the planet, we never have (or don't allow ourselves to have) a moment to tune in to our own self-discovery channel and ask what will please and delight ourselves, never mind celebrate the joys of being us.

Celebrating being you is crucial to your sense of self. Understanding that your imperfections as well as your assets combine to produce a total unique package that cannot be replicated will strengthen your self-awareness and self-esteem. Acknowledging the power of the individual sum of your parts as well as your entirety gives you colour and character. It makes you fun to be around, fascinating to other people. It will give you something with which to flesh out your memoirs. Your individual qualities give you a better chance of succeeding and being number one in your world than if you were the mirror image of someone else. There is only room for one of everyone in the world. Make sure the one of you is the true one.

Looking back at your answers to this quiz, do you see a theme emerging? Now ask yourself this: are you living a life that matches your true identity? Or are your answers in conflict with your current existence? Are you an artist living an accountant's life or an accountant living an artist's life? It's easy to find ourselves believing we are one person living one kind of life. The trick is in identifying that the life you lead is the right one for you; that it suits all the genuine sides of your personality. Use the answers you've written down as a reminder of who you are and a wake-up call to being yourself and living your life according to your own aspirations – no matter how insane they seem to other people.

When you face up to who you are and understand there's no right or wrong way to be, that just being you is a brilliant way to be, you have a whole appreciation of your sense of self and are half-way to becoming number one in your own world.

> *Being number one in your own world is about celebrating who you are, good and bad. View yourself and your life as a wonderful jigsaw that's made up of small pieces. Each piece plays an important part in making up the end result. You may not like or feel particularly proud of some of the pieces. But if one piece were missing, you wouldn't be able to create the great total picture.*
> **Jenny Swift, Director at Ketchum Life PR agency**

The New Role Model – You!

As the new sense of self emerges in the millennium, it seems to me role models should be shelved. You may think I have gone momentarily mad. But if you truly understand the concept of being number one in your own world, you'll understand that if you *are* number one in your own world, you cannot possibly model yourself on someone else. Why? Okay, I'll explain further. Modelling yourself on someone else is to want to be someone else. It means denying the incredible repertoire of characteristics that go towards making you truly special, from all your unique and fabulous assets to all your glorious and fascinating imperfections.

Every person who is successful in their own world has as many imperfections as you. What's more, I truly believe not a single one has more fabulous assets than you. So why should you want to be like anyone else? All you will be doing is swapping one cocktail of characteristics for another. Sure, admire specific qualities and certainly learn from them if you can. As you'll see already, I've peppered this book with quotes from people who have succeeded in becoming number one in their world, and I've done that for a good reason. It's smart to seek help from those who have gone before. And it's canny to learn from the successes and disappointments of people who've experienced similar journeys to the one you desire for yourself. But mould yourself into an identikit of any one of them? I'd rather you shred this book right now than read on under this misconception.

Being number one in your own world means benchmarking against nothing other than your own expectations of yourself. Being number one in your own world means succeeding on your own terms rather than those of others. Being number one in your own world means using your intuition about what feels right for you rather than adhering to others' guidelines. If you use one or two role models as icons of perfection, you will never be the one-of-a-kind you can be. You will simply be the second best.

One of my favourite articles ever to appear in *Cosmopolitan* was written by the notorious and opinionated columnist, Julie Burchill. It concerned role models and whether they were a help to young women – or a hindrance. Here's what she wrote:

The day you rip down all the posters on your bedroom wall (the sound of tearing posters is the sound of an adult individual finally emerging from the conformist chrysalis of youth) and start looking in the mirror for inspiration instead, is the day you finally get a life – yours ... Those who can, do; those who can't, gaze worshipfully at role models. Look at Margaret Thatcher – not a man to match her, and not a woman to inspire her. The Conservative party leadership was, historically, a woman-free zone – females were seen fit only, if old, to sing 'Jerusalem' and make jam for fund-raising bring 'n' buys. Or, if young, to 'get off' with after hours at Party conferences. Yet, Mrs Thatcher did it – with no path to follow and no idol to aspire to.

When I was at school, one of our favourite pastimes was discussing 'Who do you want to be like?'. At the time, Toyah Wilcox, Paula Yates and Chrissie Hynde were the most popular responses. Germaine Greer, Margaret Thatcher and Anna Ford also crept into conversation. And I believe my friend, Pamela, even said she'd love to be like the fiction writer, Jilly Cooper ... remember this *was* the late 1970s. But looking back, I can't help breathing an enormous sigh of relief that none of us actually took seriously the concept of role models. For although there were truly commendable aspects of each one of those women (some, frankly, more commendable than others), none was perfect. My personal saving grace came when I was asked to detail my aspirations on my application form for my newspaper training course. I wrote 'I don't want to be the next Harold Evans, I want to be the first Mandi Norwood'. Not an outstandingly smart piece of prose, admittedly, but it highlighted a sense of self that was far more likely to pay off than any aspiration to be like someone else.

Putting people on pedestals as paragons of perfection is not only naive, it's destructive to your sense of self in more ways than one. First, because rarely do we have more than a one-dimensional view of their success, which magnifies our own insecurities and the challenges everyone encounters in life. And second, if we ever get to meet our role model and discover they are not as perfect as we had once thought, it can leave us disillusioned and questioning: 'So what hope is there for me?'. In the same *Cosmo* issue that featured Julie Burchill, Chrissy Iley recalled meeting one of her role models, the feminist writer Erica Jong:

Years after my fascination began, I got to meet her. I turned up at her house wearing a Dolce & Gabbana Botticelli print blouse and she said she had the same one in her wardrobe. We bonded. But she then told me she had reconsidered everything she had said in the Seventies ... We became friends, sort of. But she couldn't be a role model anymore. Not a guru, not a person who always made the right choice.

Rather than pinning your aspirations on one-dimensional, abstract figurines, it's way healthier and wiser to look at a whole array of people close to you that you both like and respect for real reasons. Having mentors – people you admire for what they have achieved in their own worlds and whom you trust to give good, impartial advice – is a mature and healthy way to make your individual aspirations real. But mentors are people with tangible qualities, people who excel not only because they have confidence and passion but also in spite of their insecurities and neuroses. For instance, I have learned a sense of justice and desire for perfection from my mother, but I don't want to be like her. From my friends I have learned kindness, courage, dignity and wit, but I wouldn't want to be any of them. From work colleagues, I've learned determination, perspective, grit, commitment and passion, but would I really want to be like them? No. Yes, there are wonderful lessons to be learned from them, without having to be like them. Why would I? Would you? Why on earth would you want to be like someone else when you can be so great as you?

Which naturally brings me on to ...

CHAPTER 5

Peer Fear: Don't Let it Destroy the Real You

(and get in your way of being number one in your world)

Yes, there have never been more choices available to us — regardless of your sex, age, colour or culture. And yes, there has never been more of a chance for you to fulfil your potential and be number one in your world. So why is it that one of the oldest issues in the psychology books now threatens to whip our dreams from right under our feet and ruin our chances of truly being number one in our own world?

I'm talking of peer fear. It can also go under the heading of jealousy or envy, but this terminology is way too basic for this millennial affliction. Here's why: jealousy is something our ancestors may have felt on seeing a neighbour with a bigger buffalo steak on the fire than theirs. Envy is something Elizabeth I's sister, Mary, may have felt towards her prettier, wittier sibling, even though she was closer in succession to the throne. Jealousy or envy is what our grandparents may feel at the scope of opportunities available to us. But peer fear is the modern twist on those two basic human emotions now we have real power to change our lives and take control of our destiny.

Because with choice comes decision. And with decision comes fear you'll make a bad one ... or not as right as your peer. While on the one hand, we accept that we have the right to live out our dreams, many of us live under a cloud of fear that we're not doing our opportunities justice. We often fear that those dreams aren't as valid or as big or as meaningful as those of our peers. And that having achieved our dreams, they may not be as exciting or fulfilling as the dreams we could have fulfilled – and the dreams we see our peers fulfilling.

Oh my!

The media is filled with stories of people who have cracked up under the strain of peer fear, not only attempting to meet their own expectations, but the expectations of others as well. We read about an increasing number of teenagers who, unable to cope with standards set by their peer group, decide to end their young and promising lives. We read more stories about women and men who, unable to be the good parents/employees/employers/spouses they believe everyone else is, seek solace in behaviour which ultimately destroys their ability to function as human beings, never mind anything else.

The other side of this, of course, is that often, when we read these articles or watch programmes about them on TV, we feel relieved. They make us feel better about our own stresses. In some cases, we can use the experiences of those we read or hear about to ensure we don't come to the same sorry end; but in other cases, we can use these stories as an excuse for us not to even try going down the same road. All too often, however, we use our peers as our only benchmark, quite forgetting what it is that we really want and what we have achieved to date.

In a recent article in *Cosmopolitan* about the same subject, a wonderful young writer named Sophie Walker wrote hilariously about the debilitating effect of her experiences of peer fear. Here's what she said:

I am having a normal day. Work was good. I did have to cancel the drink I was supposed to have with a friend (too tired). But the house is relatively clean. There is food in the fridge, money in the bank and a cup of tea in my hand. Life is just fine. I sit down and turn on the television. There, on the screen, is the woman I started work experience with, on the same day, on the same publication, nine years ago. She, looking lithe and blonde, is presenting Top of the Pops. *Suddenly, in that moment, I reassess my life: it is, in fact, utterly worthless. Seeing her there makes me feel physically sick. Disappointment and the desire to throw up do battle in the pit of my stomach. I feel undermined. I thought I had a career. I suddenly realize I have nothing. I am pathetic and petty. She is my age and she is doing better than me. My life is without meaning. OK, I'm exaggerating slightly, but I can't help it. I am in the grip of peer fear — the belief that a contemporary's achievements completely negate my own.*

My flatmate Caroline stood by and watched disdainfully as I did my ritual peer fear dance. By the time I had finished striding around the living room, ranting at the top of my voice and ended by lying dejectedly on the sofa, twitching like a stuck pig, Caroline was asking if perhaps I thought I took these things a little too personally.

'Just because she's presenting Top of the Pops *doesn't mean she's better than you,' she reasoned.*

'It does,' I wailed.

'Do you think she's really happy?' Caroline asked.

'Yeeees,' I wailed.

'Right, I'm not talking to you — you're mad,' Caroline concluded.

I know she is right. In a perfect world, I know that what person X is doing, what they have and what they earn, would not affect me. But I can't help it. Jealous, I could live with. But this is worse. Five minutes ago, I loved what I had. Now I feel I don't have anything.

I've felt like this. I'm sure you have, too. Because the thing about peer fear is that it is not just about jealousy or envy or insecurity, but a powerful cocktail of all three: jealousy that we feel someone else has something we deserve instead; envy in that we want something which someone else has; and insecurity in that we feel we do not deserve to have nice things because we aren't bright or witty or attractive enough. Feeling the first two emotions in isolation can be motivating, spurring us on to work even harder. But when all three ugly sister feelings turn up at the party, we really get into trouble.

How to Be Number One in Your Own World

Peer fear can not only stop you focusing on being number one in your world (the immediate effect of it is to send your confidence levels plummeting), but it can also send you off in entirely different directions that are not just out of kilter with your own talents and strengths, but out of kilter with what you really want.

I spoke to an ex-editor at a conference recently. I was curious to find out why she'd only lasted two months in her first editorship:

I'd always loved writing and dreamed one day that I would write a novel. And after a year of applying for every job going, I finally landed a writer's position on a magazine. I was thrilled and delighted beyond my dreams. After a month, I realized that although I was one of the oldest on the magazine, I was in one of the most junior positions. It really rankled me. Then a girl I'd made friends with left to edit a teen magazine and we virtually stopped seeing each other. She was always in meetings, or at parties or on trips. The fact that I was writing tons and loved it no longer mattered. My dream of a novel went right out of the window. Instead, I thought, 'If she can be an editor and go to parties, then so can I'. One year later, I got my opportunity, my own magazine to look after. The first day was okay, but the following days and weeks turned into a nightmare. Of course, I wasn't writing any more — I was in meetings, sorting out departments, fighting over broken fax machines, motivating other people. I wasn't good at it and I didn't enjoy it. At all. I realized I'd made a dreadful mistake. What's more, my bosses realized it too. Then one morning, I woke up and just knew I couldn't go into the office.

I felt ill just thinking about it. So I phoned in, explained how I felt and finished by resigning there and then.

Since then, (I'll call her) Emma, has become a freelance writer. I know she's brilliant at it because I've read her work all over the place. And when she isn't doing what she loves for magazines and newspapers, she writes the novel she's always dreamed of. She got where she wanted to be, finally. But the lesson she learned about peer fear is a painful one: that it's okay to admire and even envy (a little) other people's positions in their world, but attempting to make their world your world (and attempting to be number one in it) is disastrous.

How to Banish Peer Fear – and be Number One in Your World

DON'T	DO
feel you're in competition with anyone else	understand in your world the only one you're in competition with is you
mistake feelings of admiration for jealousy	ask yourself, 'Do I really want the life they have?'
dwell on everyone else's achievements	celebrate every single one of your achievements

believe the grass is always greener on the other side	make a list of everything that person gives up for their success
forget the great elements of your life	write down everything in your life someone may feel envious of
equate their success with the only success there is	construct your own definition of success

Time to Change

In any of our lifetimes there has never been such a time for change: change in society's values, yes, but change in our perception of ourselves too. The start of a whole new millennium is an amazing time for us all to make the ultimate new year's resolution and maximize the self. We can leave the frightened, doubting, complacent old self behind in the 20th century. The 21st century is as new and exciting as time could possibly be which gives us a sense of momentum that has never existed before.

Say, if you must, 'I will never experience a new millennium again'. You could also say 'If I don't do it now, I never will'. Or, 'There's no time like the present'. Say just one of these sentences or say all of them. Either way, you will be right. The mood is right for change, perfect for high expectations, ideal for making dreams come true. Never has there been a better time for being number one in your own world. Don't allow the moment to pass.

> *Not being a religious person, the only message I can take away from the violent and premature loss of such dear friends, and from facing my own mortality is: Carpe diem. Seize the day. Diana [Princess of Wales] and Gianni [Versace], two vibrant human beings in the prime of life, are gone, and I am thriving. If anything, I had imagined the princess attending my memorial service, and here I was, attending hers. I don't know how to resolve this conundrum, to make peace with these ridiculous facts, except to embrace the long life she was denied.*
>
> **Quoted from *No Time To Die* by the late Liz Tilberis, Editor-in-Chief, *Harper's Bazaar***

CHAPTER 6

Self-esteem: the Truth in the Cliché

When you look at yourself, what do you see? Do you see a person who frowns or smiles a lot? Do you hear yourself laughing or complaining? Do your eyes sparkle or just, every now and then, glimmer? Do you see ugly or attractive? Do you see a package of exciting possibilities or an empty carcass?

On a scale of nought to ten, where would you place yourself? Are you happy with your position? Where would you like to be? And why are you not there? There will, undoubtedly, be many reasons why we are not happy, why we feel we are not number one in our own world but number two, three or four. And what fundamentally steers our behaviour is our attitude to life and our self. Yes, it sounds like a cliché – you may even say a magazine cliché, after all, magazines like *Cosmo* are packed with articles on the power of self-esteem – but there is truth in the cliché as anyone who is number one in their own world will tell you.

So here's a very simple rule: it is not who or what you are that shapes your life but the way you interpret your self and events that happen to you. Contrary to my belief that rules are to be broken, this is one rule that no one has ever proved can be broken. So I won't go into huge depth about it. I'm just about to offer a few simple strategies you can call on when your internal engine is feeling low in self-esteem fuel, to give you the power to move forward and get what you want.

Self-esteem Boost 1

Examine the Evidence

Imagine you've taken a step nearer to your dream by making a phone call and you totally fluff it. Afterwards you tell yourself, 'I never do anything right. I'm such a loser.' You recognize that behaviour? Of course you do. It's a classic symptom of low self-esteem and we've all been guilty of it. But when this happens to you, break the pattern by examining the evidence. Ask yourself is it really true you *never* do anything right? Never? Really? Aren't there some things you actually do quite well? Of course there are. Nobody's that bad, least of all you. Okay, this phone call didn't go that well, but this only makes you human, not a total loser. And at least you can learn from your mistakes …

How to Be Number One in Your Own World

Self-esteem Boost 2

Be Your Own Best Friend

Would you say the negative things you tell yourself to a close friend when they're feeling down? Of course not. You'd tell them how smart they are, how fun they are to be with, how great they look ... you'd highlight all their strengths and assets and you'd take delight from them blossoming again before your very eyes. So why on earth don't you behave in the same way to your very best friend – you? Most people are a lot more reasonable and generous towards other people than they are towards themselves. Give yourself some of the same treatment.

Self-esteem Boost 3

Be Convinced of Your Worth

When I was a little girl, I absolutely loathed, like most little girls, spiders, flies, earwigs (*especially* earwigs). I remember saying to my dad, 'I hate bugs and flies, I wish they didn't exist. What's the point of them? They don't do anything.' My dad was a biology teacher so he was bound to give this great answer: 'Everything is put on the planet for a purpose. If flies didn't exist, spiders wouldn't have anything to eat. And if spiders didn't exist, there would be tons of flies.' I didn't like creepy crawlies any more for this explanation, but I've never forgotten the point: if flies (and even earwigs!) have a value, then I must certainly be valuable, even if some days I feel no better than a measly bug. One of my colleagues, Liz Kershaw, publishing director of *Cosmopolitan*, has tons of energy and self-esteem. When I asked her how she maintains her motivation and self-esteem even on down-days, she came back with this retort:

If I wake up in the morning feeling low, I give myself a pinch and tell myself 'Hey, you're a great person and there's a whole world full of people out there just dying to meet you!'

(Note to readers: I've tried this when I've felt shy or vulnerable before entering a room full of strangers – and it works!) If your life feels pointless and you feel worthless, remember everything and everyone has a value – make sure you remember yours and then tell the world.

Self-esteem Boost 4

Talk the Talk Positive
Don't let that critical chatterbox consume your thoughts. Replace it with positive applause ... and repeat ... and repeat ... and repeat. Go on, give it a try; you may feel

How to Be Number One in Your Own World

self-conscious but talking the talk is critical to driving up your self-esteem. Tell yourself 'I'm great. I'm great! I'm GREAT!' At first, you don't have to believe what you're saying – although it helps. But, like a catchy radio jingle, if you hear something often enough, it sets up shop in your subconscious. On top of that, talking positively to yourself boosts your energy and helps you move forward. You can also write down your positive statements 20 times a day, concentrating on your goal. Or record on cassette tape your declarations and listen to them in your car. Or turn them into your computer screen-saver and stare at them umpteen times during the day.

Self-esteem Boost 5

Turn up the Volume on Positive Thoughts (and Turn Down the Volume on Negative Ones)

Only you think the bad thoughts running through your head, so you have the power to control them. The real power in your life is with you, the manufacturer of your thoughts, not the thoughts themselves. Once you recognize this, you open the door to new options. So when you find yourself having a negative thought about yourself, say 'Here I go again, thinking negatively. I'm not going to fall into this trap any more.' And then follow with 'I'm bright and I'm free and I can do it.'

Self-esteem Boost 6

Act as if ...

Assume the posture you would have if you felt the way you want to feel. Dress the way you'd dress if you were in the role you wanted to be in. Talk the way you'd talk if you *were* number one in your own world. When you act like you're confident and valued and happy, sooner or later, it no longer becomes an act. You will be number one in your own world!

I certainly don't get up in the morning and think 'I don't do things well.' I get up in the morning and think 'I do things rather better than some.'

Felicity Kendal, actress

CHAPTER 7

How to Get to Number One

How far have you come since you started this book? I know you were on the road to being number one in your own world because you bought this book and had the courage to open the first page. You want to be number one in your own world? Of course you do – because it's the best place to be. It makes you feel glad to be alive, that your life has meaning, direction and focus.

Here's a secret: I've asked myself periodically 'If my life were a film, would it inspire others to live a life similar to mine; would the audience be cheered by or depressed by the events and outcomes in the plot; would they find me a pathetic character to be pitied, scorned or loathed or would they admire me and respect my achievements, even if they didn't much like me?' Hey, I'm not saying I've lived my life for the approval of others – are you kidding? But sometimes it's worth attempting to view your aspirations and achievements objectively, from a distance, because this way you can truly appreciate them. I've often missed things I've achieved because I've been so close to them. It's taken someone else to point out their merit before I've been able to acknowledge that they are achievements of which I should be proud. Weird isn't it?

So let's get down to business. During the course of this crucial chapter, I will attempt to crystallize some strategies I have used to help me focus on what I want, and to encourage me when it seemed just too difficult or too much hassle to go on.

You've come this far, now GO FOR IT!

Dream Your Dream

Cast your mind back to when you were eight, nine or ten. Re-create the fantasies you had as a child. What did you want to be when you grew up? Perhaps you wanted to be a great singer, an airline pilot, a train driver, an artist, a poet. Don't laugh. Now you're all grown up, it doesn't mean you shouldn't tap into the very things that excited you on a basic level.

These childhood dreams may not necessarily reflect what you want to be right now, but what they embody is your emotional desires. As you know, when I was eight or nine, I wanted to be a ballerina. Frankly, the idea now appalls me. For a start, there's not enough money in it. Also, as I developed into a woman, I realized that my physique was not cut out for ballet, unless I wanted to dance the part of a matron in *Cinderella* or *Sleeping Beauty*.

But, looking back with my adult head on, I now realize those dreams of being a ballerina were my way of expressing my need for a starring role in whatever I chose to be. They showed even then, in those immature years, that I was desperate to be creative, work with beautiful images and give them to an appreciative audience. They signified a need for applause, a need for glamour and sparkle and a desire to work with other people in the creation of something that transports its audience into another world.

My dreams of being a ballerina took me to far-off lands, not just to the end of the road where I lived in my home town. They represented my need to be challenged and work hard. They also reflected my competitive streak, even then, because in my dreams I was not a member of the corps de ballet; I was the prima ballerina, pirouetting solo on an empty stage, until, with a final fabulous flourish, I would leap into the arms of the male principal dancer to a thunder of rapturous applause.

Of course, some years later, I decided the nitty-gritty of being a ballerina was not what I wanted at all. In actual fact, there are some elements of ballet that really irritate me now I'm a ballet-watching adult, and I doubt I would have reconciled my irritation with a career in it. But the basic tenets of my early dream have remained: the need for challenge, glamour, applause, travel, competition.

What were your dreams? No matter how ridiculous or fantastical they seem now, give yourself time to wallow in them, imagine yourself doing them now and the great things (as well as the not so great things) they would give you at this stage in your life. You dreamed of being a vet or a doctor? Great! (I chose this because there's hardly a single person I know who didn't go through that phase.) Try if you can to analyse now what it was about that dream that you loved. A longing to help, to be respected, to work hard, to make a difference, to work within a community, to be needed?

Write your dreams down on one side of a sheet of paper and, on the other side, what it was about the dream that so made you buzz. I know that the reasons you wanted to be a vet or a doctor (or the prime minister or an actress or jewellery designer or whatever) will correspond with what you want today. Remember, we hardly change as we grow up. In fact, those basic needs just become stronger and stronger as we mature.

You probably had two or three dreams that took you through childhood and adolescence. If you did, write them down and examine them one by one. Chances are, there are similarities in those dreams. Those similarities may be very loose – for instance, a need to work with other people or to make lots of money or behave outrageously – but the more you analyse and write down, the more you will build a picture of what it is you really wanted from life – and, very probably, what you (perhaps even secretly) want from your life right now.

Your Dreams Now

Having studied your earliest dreams, it's time to write down what your dreams are right now. Go on — allow yourself this indulgence … actually, it's not an indulgence, although we're brought up to dismiss daydreaming in this way ('Oh, I haven't the time to daydream'). Dreaming is a way of waking up to possibilities. Without daydreams, the lottery would founder. Without dreams, Martin Luther King would not have been one of the greatest human rights activists of the last century (remember his famous opening 'I have a dream …'?). Very little in this world happens purely by chance. Everything starts with a dream.

Three Steps to Dreaming Your Dreams
Step 1
Here are the ingredients you need to start the dreaming process. They're quite simple:

- a glass of wine
- a chair in the garden, by the fire, by a window
- music that inspires you
- solitude or a non-judgemental companion (dog, cat, rabbit or person)

Imagine, consider, write down or vocalize what you would do if the world was your oyster, if you could do absolutely anything. Put aside practical obstacles for a moment, such as no money, family responsibilities, lack of qualifications or training. Just let your imagination meander. Don't feel inhibited …this isn't about who can have the most outrageous dream, it's about YOUR dream, what you would want in an ideal world.

Make a mental or written list. Why not include:

- Where you would go.
- What you would see.
- Who you would meet.
- How you would spend your time.
- Who you would like to share this dream with.
- A big smiling picture of you, pasted in the centre of your dream map.

Allow yourself time to do this. Perhaps you won't be able to do it all in one sitting. After all, this pattern of behaviour will probably be out of character. Come back to it if you need to. You can even laugh at it and have fun. The most important thing is to do it, then weave its presence into your daily life – pin it to your fridge or memo board at home, stick it in the most-used part of your Filofax or carry it in your bag.

Step 2
Having made your dream list, it's time to scratch beneath the surface. Take each answer, and analyse it.

Where would you go? Maybe you've thought of a specific place or just somewhere with basic characteristics.

If you've answered that your dream takes place in St Tropez, ask yourself: is it really St Tropez or does St Tropez simply embody what you want from your surroundings – sea, fresh air, glamour, sunshine, a French accent?

When you asked yourself what would you see, did you imagine old buildings, familiar faces, countryside, hustle and bustle, bright lights, water, children, white walls or chintz, antiques or modern furnishings?

Who would you meet? Would it be like-minded people or people whose lives were very different from yours? Would you, perhaps, prefer not to meet anyone at all?

How would you spend your time? Would you live at a fast or slow pace? Would you play the piano by an open window overlooking the sea? Would you be rolling up your sleeves and getting stuck into local life? Would you be helping or being an onlooker? Would you be writing, singing, walking, surfing, riding, selling, making or spending money or both? Imagine your perfect day in your dream place. Write down the time you would get up, what you would have for breakfast, how you would fill your morning, where you would have lunch, what you would have for lunch, who you would have lunch with, what time you'd finish and then what you would do in the afternoon. What would make you smile during your day? What would disappoint or exhilarate or anger you? How would you end your day? What would you have wanted to accomplish? What would send you off to sleep in your dream world with a smile on your face? And who would you be sleeping next to?

Now, who would you like to share this dream with? Don't feel guilty if your dream doesn't include those with whom you presently share your life. Remember, this is about you and what you want. You're thinking purely of number one right now. Okay? You're allowed to. This is your own dream, no one else's. Whose face would you like to see first thing in the morning and last thing at night? Who would you like to meet during your dream day – don't worry if you can't name names, just write down their characteristics. What sort of people would you *not* like to encounter? Who would you like to spend most time with and who would you like to make the odd appearance?

Step 3

By now, your dream will be fairly detailed. If you've gone over it a couple of times, you may start to feel prickles of guilt or responsibility creeping into the picture. Try not to let them. We're talking, for the moment, about dreams, not reality. In your dreams, you never feel guilty (that's a nightmare!) because you are surrounded by happiness and people who appreciate what you do for them and understand why if you don't.

The third part of your dream picture is for the 'whys?'. Here goes …

Why did you choose the location for your dream? Why did you say St Tropez or Manchester or Scotland or Cape

How to Be Number One in Your Own World

Town or LA? What was it about those places that inspired you to dream about them? Perhaps they remind you of where you grew up? Perhaps they embody everything that is different to your life right now? Maybe they signify danger or challenge? Or peace and tranquillity? It could simply be that in your dream destination it's always sunny or, perhaps, cold? Try and work out why you chose that place over anywhere else in the world.

Now ask yourself why you want to see what you dreamed you would see? Why do you want to be surrounded by old buildings? Maybe you're just inspired by them or interested in them. Do you connect with the stability they represent in the world and history? Or why did you answer that you would see countryside and blue sky, but very few people? Do your responsibilities right now make you feel claustrophobic, hankering for freedom? Or do you feel uplifted and inspired when you're surrounded by greenery? Do you long for the country because you find city life too stressful or frightening or fast? Or do you imagine in your day-to-day dream life you would see familiar surroundings, shops you love, monuments you passed as a child, parks and boating lakes? If so, why? Do they remind you of happy times?

And who would you meet? Do you dream of meeting influential figures or celebrities? If so, why? Try not to answer 'Oh, just because they're interesting people …'. Instead, ask yourself why they're interesting people to you and how you would feel once you had met them or what you would say to them? Or perhaps you'd like to meet a fantastic new lover who would sweep you off your feet? Why is that? Are you unhappy in your relationship ... not necessarily unhappy even, just slightly bored, or frustrated or irritated? What would the characteristics of this person be, how would they look, how would they treat you, what would you do together, laugh about, argue over? And once you've thought about those answers, ask yourself again, why? why? why? Maybe you'd like to meet a whole new set of people with different views, different lives to what you've been used to? Why? Because you want to be a part of something new or you'd like to help as well as learn from them?

Now take a look at how you've described your dream day. Don't be afraid to go into detail. Why would you eat that for breakfast? Because it's your favourite or because it's different to what you eat right now or perhaps because eating this particular dish represents time on your hands to appreciate the flavours ... or does it represent lack of time and the busy, busy life you aspire to? See how the simple daydreaming process of what you would like to eat for breakfast can unfold into so much more about you and your life? How did you imagine you would spend your morning? Racing from one end of a city to another? Why? Because you crave the rush you get from adrenalin, you enjoy juggling more than one task at a time, and making snap decisions gives you a buzz? Or do you imagine a morning of solitude where you are able to think and create? Maybe you do. If so, why? And why do you really dream about giving a piano recital in front of an audience if you can't play an instrument to save your life? It may not make much sense to you, but if you keep on asking yourself why, you will drill right down to one or two basic answers. Even if it's that you have always fantasized about playing the piano, then that is a great and valid answer!

And finally, with whom did you want to share your dream day? Why did you envisage spending it with your boss or a new man or woman? Why, if you love your current partner, does he or she not figure in your dream? Often the answers to these questions will surprise us. We may, for instance, have daydreamed about spending our dream day with a parent who drives us crazy. Why is that? Because, secretly, you adore their company or wish you could create a relationship that doesn't currently exist? Ask yourself why you have decided that, in your dream day, no one you know makes an appearance. Is that because they undermine you or patronize you? Do you feel inhibited in their company? Is it because, in your dreams, you would reinvent yourself, start afresh with people who had never known you or could judge you based on past experiences? Asking yourself why you have included some people and not others is enlightening when in your real day you feel pressured to mingle with the same crowd.

Step 4

Now you have allowed yourself to look at your past and present dreams, you'll be surprised at the similarities. They may not be obvious, but look for matching words, images, activities. This will define what your real world is. Not necessarily the world in which you presently live, but the world in which you want to be number one.

Okay, so you can leave it at that; leave your dream world on sheets of A4, hidden under bills and books you've never got around to reading. Or you can regard them as your life hence. Remember, it's up to you. You are in control. You can do whatever you want to do.

Can you take the next step? Of course YOU CAN.

> *God didn't have time to make a nobody. As a result, you can have, or be, anything you want.*
> **Mary Kay Ash, founder of the Mary Kay Ash beauty empire**

Planning Your Dream

Often our dreams can seem so extravagant, so beyond the realms of possibility, that even to think of them sends us scuttling back into our corner. After all, it's easier to stick with what we know than to take that leap into the unknown, especially if the life we are living and the life we want to live are a million miles apart. But you know what? Every little leap you take brings you one step nearer to your dream world. But you can't take those little leaps if you don't have even a vague idea of what you want to leap on to.

So where do you go from here? Well, right back to your dream picture for starters ...

Drilling to the Heart of Your Dream

Now you have created your dream picture, it's time to dissect it. To plan effectively, you have to prioritize. You must separate the black-and-white from the colour, the black-and-white being the concrete action, the colour being the lovely, glorious detail.

Go through your dream picture with a highlighter pen and pick out the really important aspects. I'm not telling you how many you should highlight – only you can do that. But are the people in your dream more important than the location? Are they equally important? Is it vital you live in the country, or could you do what you want to do in the city? Would you be able to handle better the people you feel patronize you or demoralize you if only you could attain other aspects of your dream? If so, you possibly don't need to run away from them to a different planet, just make changes to the planet you already live on to enable you to feel better about yourself and less conscious of their irritating behaviour.

Your dream picture may be full of contradictions. Well, so is life. That doesn't matter. What matters is prioritizing what is most important to you. I've always found that when you sort out the main points, the details take care of themselves.

Procrastination is the Thief of Time ...

It's wonderful to have dreams, of course it is. And now you have your dream picture, there's no stopping you making those dreams reality. Oh yes, there is just one thing stopping you. YOU. You may well be stopping yourself right now by thinking 'When I get X sorted, I will ...' or 'Perhaps next year, I will ...' or 'Now is not the right time to ...'. Whatever variation of this theme you're thinking, what you're really doing is NOTHING. Which means time is passing you by. Every day you put off your dreams, you are denying yourself the happiness and fulfilment you deserve.

Hot, young (23 at the time of writing) fashion designer Shoshanna Lonstein's don't-wait attitude has taken her to the top of her industry in what seems like the blink of an eye. She's super-talented, of course, but so are a hundred other designers which is why she says:

Don't wait around for the perfect day to go after your goal, because it will never come — you'll always have too many other things to do and too many other people to make happy. You have to start small and put more into it every day.

Shoshanna's dead right. Don't allow the passing of time to dilute your enthusiasm for the life you want to lead. Grab this day, this hour, this minute. Make this moment the moment you will always remember as the moment your life changed. Write down that great idea NOW. Send off that letter NOW. Make that crucial appointment NOW. Say yes – or no – NOW. Pick up the phone right this moment.

Can you put a price on 24 hours of happiness? No you can't. So why put off something that's priceless? There is nothing to be gained from procrastinating. And everything to lose. Waiting until this fictional right time to do something doesn't make it all the sweeter when you do it. It just means you've lost time savouring the wonderful taste of it. The right time to do anything is not tomorrow or the next day. When you know you need to take action for your happiness, the right time is always NOW.

One of the most successful businesswomen in the world, Linda Wachner, turned cosmetic company Max Factor around at the grand young age of 33 with a very simple philosophy: Do It Now. From losing $16 million a year, she stemmed the haemorrhaging of the American division in her first year and was able to produce a $5 million operating profit in her second. She then gave a repeat performance with Max Factor worldwide within the same time frame. She so believed in the Do It Now philosophy, it became the Max Factor motto – in fact, she had it inscribed in large letters on the cover of every memo pad and notebook in the company and gave one to all her employees. Procrastination? Pah!

Not so long ago I met Julie, 34, who is a researcher on a popular TV chat show. She told me that because she was feeling frustrated and dissatisfied with her life, she thought she might look at opportunities in America, perhaps write a few letters to some networks, make a couple of phone calls. 'Great!' I said. 'When?'

'Oh, not until next year. I just don't feel confident doing it this year,' Julie replied.

'Why?' I asked. 'What do you hope will happen this year that will make you confident enough to make inroads into America next year?'

'Ah, good question,' laughed Julie.

I asked Julie why she didn't just send off a handful of letters right now, just to see what happened. 'After all,' I suggested, 'if anything does happen – if anyone makes you an offer or writes back with an invitation to visit – you don't *have* to take it. Also, if you leave it until next year, there will be more competition from another year's worth of college leavers. And who's to say you really will feel more confident in a year? You may well feel less confident because you're more frustrated and dissatisfied than ever.'

If Julie does send off a handful of letters, she can't lose. Even if she receives a handful of rejections in return, she's no worse off than she is right now. And she can still make contact again next year, when, who knows, there may be a different recruitment manager or recruitment policy, or someone may remember Julie from her first letter and admire her persistence. On the other hand, Julie may just strike gold this year – she certainly stands a better chance than if she doesn't give it a go until next year. And the

How to Be Number One in Your Own World

added bonus is, she may have saved herself 12 months of misery by not procrastinating.

> *My parents were influential on my attitude to getting what I wanted. They taught me that you're only on this planet once. The best advice they gave me was 'Don't hang about. Get cracking.'*
>
> **Deborah Warwick Jones, chiropodist**

Building a Bridge Between Dream and Reality

Now imagine you need to build a bridge between present and future. What do you need in order to build that bridge? I'm no carpenter, but let's imagine you need wood, a saw, nails, a screwdriver, a hammer. These are the basic tools required to start the job.

What do *you* need to do to get started? Make a contact? Send a letter? Sign up for a course? Book a flight? Write a synopsis? Buy a book? See a doctor? Borrow a sewing machine? Make a list of everything you would need to start your engine, then with a full tool box, you have the confidence you only get from feeling fully equipped to take action.

> *If you have a dream, vocalize it, tell people about it. I've always been amazed by how willing people are to help. Inevitably, someone you tell will be able to help make achieving your dream that bit easier, or at least they'll know someone who knows someone else who can. It isn't a cop-out, it's smart.*

> *Keeping dreams to yourself cuts you off from potentially useful resources. Those who have achieved their dreams have always done so with a little help from other people.*
>
> **Leah Hardy, Executive Creative Editor,**
> *Cosmopolitan*

Don't be afraid to seek out advice, ask for or take help when it's offered. Make contact with others who've achieved something similar to what you want to achieve. I have found that even the loftiest people respond with pride when you ask how they did it. (It makes them feel soooo important.) It makes me feel very important when wannabe editors ask 'How did you get to be Editor of *Cosmopolitan*?' But the answer, I'm sure, is always a mixture of disappointment and inspiration because it is basically so straightforward. So you don't have to spend another day collecting information to pursue your dream by asking me how I pursued mine, I'll tell you quickly …

I started with a dream, just about got through A levels, then applied for a course in newspaper journalism. It seemed quite logical that, to be a journalist, I'd need to go on a course to learn how. When I discovered I preferred the idea of working on a magazine to working on a paper, I found out where all the magazines were based, and since I had no friends or relatives who could help me open doors, I reckoned the only way I was going to land a job on a magazine was if I muscled my way into that environment. So, having applied for a course, I booked my seat on the coach from Newcastle to London for another September start. Two weeks in, it seemed that more or less everyone on the course, except me, knew someone who'd give them a leg up into magazines. So no two ways about it ... letters had to be written and sent to magazines I most wanted to work for, begging and pleading with them to give me some work experience. After many rejections, one brave young magazine (*Look Now*, sadly no longer in existence) took me on for two weeks ... Eight weeks later (following irate letters from my college from where I had been absent for way too long), I was offered a job and so it happened. Without sounding horribly blasé about it (because I'm definitely not ... I can still remember the tears of frustration and agonizing bouts of self-doubt), it was that simple. But when you get down to it, it happened because I went on a course, wrote a letter, booked a coach seat, and turned up promptly. Yes, I worked hard. But I wasn't a genius. Far from it. I just made sure I amassed the tools I needed to make my dreams possible. Later I will tell you how I climbed the ladder from my first job in magazines to becoming Editor of *Cosmo*.

Set Yourself Realistic Targets

When people have high aspirations, they often call them dreams. They categorize them in fantasy terms because those aspirations seem so huge and so unachievable. After all, don't dreams only exist in the mind? Well, yes, they do if that's where you choose to keep them. But dreams can become reality if you break them down into small chunks. Those small chunks by themselves don't appear to be very significant at all, but combined, they become a dream fulfilled.

I remember the first time I drove on my own from London to Newcastle to see my parents for Christmas. As the day approached, I had butterflies in my stomach. It seemed such a long way to drive on my own. What if I got lost? Took a wrong turning? Had a flat tyre? Broke down? Where would I stop to eat? Oh hell, it seemed easier to take the train, and it probably would have been, but I really really wanted to drive. It had become a small symbol of my adulthood.

I asked my mother to send me very specific directions, which I then broke down into half a dozen points, starting with: drive up the Finchley Road through north London until you see signs for the M1. Suddenly this long drive ahead of me didn't seem so daunting. That said, I still climbed into my car with sweating palms and a fuzzy head. I remember saying under my breath, 'Mandi, if you can just find and get on to the M1, you'll be fine.' And, boy, when I saw that first M1 road sign, the sense of jubilation was incredible. Anyone would have thought I'd discovered Inca treasure. But better was to come ... I was almost dizzy with relief and self-congratulation as I put my foot down for that first leg of the motorway. Not only had I completed phase one of my journey, but I was well on the way with phase two. I know this probably sounds mad but, hey, that's how I felt. By the time I pulled up to my parents' house, however, I was thoroughly blasé about the whole experience. Drive from London to Newcastle? Simple pimple! Anyone can do that. But the point is, those small achievements along the way had encouraged me to carry on. As I completed every phase of my journey, my confidence grew until I was so relaxed, I was able to sing loudly along to the radio without fearing for my life. In fact, I really enjoyed the experience. Now, of course, I zoom up to the north and back down again without a second's thought. Mission accomplished.

And you know what? When I received the commission to write this book (and it has always been my dream to write a book), I experienced that same rush of fear and panic. What? Sixty thousand words? Are you kidding? There's no way I could possibly write a book of 60,000 words. Best to keep the book where it belongs ... in dream land.

Thankfully, for over-populated dream land, I had already signed the contract, so I had to get on with it. But I can't tell you how many times I just sat staring at my computer, overwhelmed by the sheer enormity of the task ahead. So here's what I did ... Well, first I put the kettle on and made a cup of tea. Then I shuffled a few papers around. Then I decided to tidy my study ... after all, if I put everything into order around me, I'd feel more efficient. So I dusted and filed and flicked through magazines and vacuumed. Then I switched on the radio and switched it off again. And then I changed what I was wearing. Maybe if I put my lucky suit on, good fortune would prevail with a blast of inspiration and creativity. What happened? Nothing. I was still me, except now I was sitting in a spotless study in my lucky suit! The dream had become a nightmare.

I trudged downstairs, despondent, demoralized and feeling like an utter twerp. Who on earth was I to even think I could write a book? So I made another cup of tea and watched TV. Yes, that was better ... I felt cosy now. After all, I didn't need to write this book. The world wouldn't stop spinning, would it? But slowly, as the cartoons on TV danced before my eyes, I began to feel I was compromising my potential. How much would I regret this if I gave up before I'd even begun? So, in front of the singing telly, I wrote a plan. How would I start? What would I call my first chapter? Where would that lead me? What if I broke this big idea down into ten smaller parts? Suddenly, it was looking less ominous. Yes, I thought, I can write about self-esteem. I think and talk about it every day on *Cosmo*. And yes, I can get something on paper about having a dream. I've had dreams since I can remember.

So back upstairs I ran, switched on my computer and typed in my ten rough ideas for chapters. Wow! How good did that feel? At last, I'd put something down on paper. I hadn't come anywhere near finishing the book, but, phew!

I'd made a start. As I've begun and completed each part of this book, I've put a great big tick next to every task on my list, and the sense of satisfaction is enormous.

How to Make a Task List

- Imagine your ultimate goal and consider every step you need to take in order to achieve your goal.
- If each individual task still seems too great, break it down into sub-tasks. Every task you set needs to be achievable.
- When you complete each task, do something to commemorate its completion. Personally, just etching a great big tick next to my task list is enough to give me a buzz. But I've also bought myself rewards, from a Cadbury's Creme Egg to a new CD. It's so important to celebrate each step you've taken closer to your dream.
- If you find you have a mental block or don't have the tools to complete a task, don't be afraid to skip onto one you know you can achieve in the near future to give you the confidence or time to go back to the other one.

SMART Moves

When businesses plan how to achieve budgets and goals, they do so with a SMART plan:

S – sustainable

M – measurable

A – achievable

R – realistic

T – targets

This is a great way of defining your own personal tasks. Ask yourself:

- 'Can I *sustain* the commitment required to complete this task?' If you believe you can't, break the task down into smaller tasks so you *can* sustain your commitment to them. If you dream of being an advertising copywriter, say, and sending off letters to all the agencies is getting you nowhere fast, it's natural to feel your commitment to your dream waning. Few of us can sustain our energy and commitment in the face of constant rejection. However, you could decide to obtain a couple of weeks' unpaid work experience in your holiday at an agency – most companies are only too happy to embrace a free workforce, and it could do wonders for your sense of achievement, as well as looking great on your CV. As well as that, you could enrol on a part-time or evening course at a local college. Again, being accepted will boost your commitment to your long-term dream as well as provide you with the extra ammunition you need to sustain your commitment to your long-term task of your dream advertising job. Get the picture?

- 'Can my achievements be *measured*?' If they are taking you one step nearer to your dream, then this is a measure of the success of your task. For instance, you want to be an actor. Obtaining an agent is a measurable

How to Be Number One in Your Own World

achievement you can be proud of. As is landing a part in a local production.

- 'Is this task *achievable*?' If your task simply is not achievable, no matter what you do, think again. You may wish to sail around the world, but without a boat, it simply isn't possible. Again, break that dream down into smaller tasks, then it may just become achievable. Save £100, learn how to sail, make contact with other people who share your dream, get a list of possible sponsors and so on. See how you can begin to touch even the most unattainable.

- 'Is it *realistic*?' You may say I'm contradicting myself by asking you to consider the realism of your aspirations. But reality does play a part. No point dreaming about taking a holiday to Mars when the practical reality does not exist. Does not exist *yet*. Okay, that's extreme. But, for instance, I have a dream that I'm arranging flowers and baking scones in a little cottage in a remote part of Ireland. My reality is that I would go doo-lally after six weeks of isolated scone-baking. You know what I'm saying...

- 'Do I have a *target*?' Keep in mind the validity of every target you set as well as your overall target. Each of your targets or tasks has meaning.

> *Whenever I need some self-encouragement, I make lists of things I need to do, but I always include things which I have already done so that I immediately feel better. When I'm stressed, I make a list, eat some cake, go for a swim.*
>
> **Ann McPherson, GP and author (*The Diary of a Teenage Health Freak*)**

Learn to Say 'I Can'

> *When we were established as a mail order record company, and thus dependent on the post, out of the blue came a six month postal strike. If we hadn't reinvented ourselves, we would have gone bust. There was no choice. Within days of the strike, we had opened our first Virgin Records shop. It may have been up a dark, narrow flight of stairs above a shoe shop and have consisted merely of some shelves, a shabby sofa and a till, but in its own small way, it taught us all we now know about retailing. I can draw a straight line between that tiny shop and the Virgin Megastores in Paris and New York. It's just a matter of scale. But first you have to believe you can make it happen.*
>
> **Richard Branson, entrepreneur, from his autobiography, *Losing My Virginity***

Here's a quiz. Place a tick in either the can or can't box next to each statement.

People can (i.e. have the ability to…):   CAN   CAN'T

	CAN	CAN'T
Walk on the moon	☐	☐
Drive at 160 miles per hour	☐	☐
Swim the English Channel	☐	☐
Rebuild cities	☐	☐
Transplant hearts	☐	☐
Read when they are blind	☐	☐
Save almost-certain goals	☐	☐
Build tunnels under the sea	☐	☐
Speak ten languages fluently	☐	☐
Give birth	☐	☐
Stop smoking	☐	☐
Run a mile in under four minutes	☐	☐
Compose music	☐	☐
Make a million pounds	☐	☐
Escape captivity	☐	☐

You've put a tick in every CAN box, right? Because every-thing on that list can be done by an ordinary human being. Some take years of preparation, others simply require a snap decision; some require a group of ordinary human beings, while others can be completed in isolation. Whatever … my point is, if ordinary people can achieve all the above, there is absolutely nothing *you* can't do.

Think about that letter you've always meant to send or the phone call you've always intended to make. Perhaps your hand has hovered by the postbox as you've agonized over 'Can I really send this?' As for the life-changing phone call, yes, you may have dialled the number, then slammed down the receiver with an 'Oh no, I can't' just before your call was answered. It isn't unusual to feel this way. God knows, I've experienced it myself, tearing up the letter in the middle of the street before throwing it in the nearest bin or, with pounding heart, clicking the off-button on the phone just before I'm forced to speak.

Of course, to us, these seem like enormous undertakings, but try and get them into perspective. If someone can run a mile in four minutes, you can run out and post that letter. If someone can give birth, you can make a phone call. If someone can rebuild a city, you can formulate a plan. If someone can transplant a heart, you can make a small but significant change in your life or attitude.

You see, you CAN. And believing you CAN is the most crucial step you can take in being number one in your own world. But only you can decide whether you say I can or I can't. And you have that choice. You can decide whether to take the leap or stay where you are. Whatever you do, remember you have taken the decision. Saying 'No, I can't' isn't ducking out of making a decision. It's as much of a decision as saying 'Yes, I can' and, though you may not think it, requires the same amount of strength, courage and resolve. So if you have the strength, courage and resolve to say 'I can't', you can sure as anything say 'I can'.

How to Be Number One in Your Own World

Why You Tell Yourself You Can't

We don't often rationalize why it is we tell ourselves 'I can't'. But understanding why we do often helps to turn can'ts into cans. Tick the ones that apply to you:

I can't because ...

1 I'm frightened of the unknown.
2 I may get a result which, in my heart, I don't really want.
3 I am anxious the result may not live up to my expectations.
4 I am anxious I may not live up to my or their expectations of me.
5 If it gets a result, I won't be able to change my mind.
6 I may upset those around me.
7 I don't think I am worthy.
8 It may lead to other changes in my life which I am not equipped to deal with.

How to Turn Can't into Can

Let's look at the reasons why you have told yourself you can't – and how you can turn them into 'I can'.

1 'I can't because ... I'm frightened of the unknown.'
Think about it. You want to make a change, no matter how small, to your life because there's some element of the life you know which dissatisfies you. So the 'known life' isn't perfect, right? So I ask, what have you to lose? Answer: nothing. But you have everything to gain.

2 'I can't because … I may get a result which, in my heart, I don't really want.'

Well, something may happen which you don't really want, yet something may happen which you decide you do want. If you say 'I can't', you'll never know.

3 'I can't because … I am anxious the result may not live up to my expectations.'

If the result doesn't live up to your expectations, then at least you know the life you lead right now is preferable to the alternative. What's more, rarely is a decision irreversible – unless, of course, the decision you made was to have a baby, but I have not once come across a parent who wholeheartedly regrets their decision to have a child. Back to other decisions, though: yes, the grass sometimes isn't greener on the other side. However, sometimes it is. And you'll often discover flowers, too.

4 'I can't because … I am anxious I may not live up to my or their expectations of me.'

Listen, most people go through bouts of agonizing self-doubt. In some respects, it's healthy as it makes self-doubters work harder and, thus, excel. Accept there will be times when you'll feel you are struggling, but remember, others are feeling this way, too. Whatever you do, don't allow your self-doubt to prevent you from grasping opportunities. The first step is to say 'I can'. We'll deal with your anxieties later *(see Chapter 8, page 137).*

5 'I can't because ... if it gets a result, I can't change my mind.'
Er ... why not? Show me the book which says this is so. Far better to explore the possibilities and then reject them. At least, then, you are in control, rather than the unknown controlling you. You want to move to another part of the country? You *can*. If you don't like it, you *can* always change your mind and move back to familiar territory. Fancy a different job with more responsibility and opportunity? Apply, go for an interview, even agree terms. You can always change your mind and decide to stay put. Should you ditch the relationship you're in? You can. And if the result makes you unhappy, you can always attempt to get back together on terms you're happier with. (Hey, I know from the letters I receive at *Cosmo*, this happens all the time.) If he or she won't have you back, you may well ask, was the bond between you as strong as it ought to be?

6 'I can't because ... I may upset those around me.'
Okay, it boils down to this: whose happiness is more important? Yours or theirs? The truth is, if those whom you are afraid of upsetting truly love and value you, they will accept your decision and learn to cope. What's more, your happiness doesn't have to be at the expense of the happiness of others. Don't confuse someone's inconvenience with a declaration of upset. Often, it only requires minor adjustments to ensure all parties are happy. However, it's worth asking yourself this: if those whom you are afraid of upsetting can only be happy at the expense of *your*

happiness, are they worth making the sacrifice for? I certainly could not be happy knowing someone I cared for was unhappy because of my negative attitudes to their dream. Could you?

7 *'I can't because ... I don't think I am worthy.'*
Turn straight back to the section in Chapter 1 on 'Permission to Dream' *(page 11)*. And let me stress again: everyone, regardless of sex, age, class or religion, is entitled to make changes in their life that will make them happier, feel more valued, maximize their potential. It is your right. You owe it to yourself. Now turn straight to the exercises for boosting your self-esteem in Chapter 6 *(page 78)* to give you the extra ammo you need to banish this irritating little thought that has the power to destroy your life.

8 *'I can't because ... it may lead to other changes in my life which I am not equipped to deal with.'*
Remember when I talked about breaking large dreams down into smaller, bite-sized chunks? This is just what you could do right now. And isn't it true that before a baby starts to run, she does so by learning how to take one wobbly little step at a time? Concentrate on the immediate challenge before using up your energy worrying about challenges in the future. And as you say, 'I can't because it *may...*', it means that it also may not. If it does, then simply start right back at the beginning of this book to help

you deal with these new changes. There is a fifty-fifty chance, however, that you will not need to!

Why You Should Tell Yourself You Can

■ It puts you, not others, in control of your destiny.

■ Because cans CAN.

■ Being number one in your own world is a proactive process and can is proactive (while can't is static).

■ You have nothing to lose, and everything to gain.

■ Saying you can is a declaration of your belief in your-self. When you say it, it becomes true.

When Others Make You Believe You Can't

Taking heed of those who say you can't means you are allowing others to control your destiny and your happiness. You are allowing them to take a higher position in your world than you. They may be happy about your decision based on their beliefs, but will you be? The answer is always no. How can you be happy when you have allowed someone else to define what your world is and how you should exist within that world? It's only a fabulous recipe for life if you enjoy feeling regretful, resentful, compromised and miserable.

During all my research for this book, which has involved reading about and talking with people who have achieved the fabulous status of being number one in their world, I have been amazed by how many (I'd say 90 per cent of them) have been told by others, 'You can't'.

Actually, I used to think I was a relatively rare case. (I'm thinking now of the teacher back in my comprehensive school who, due to his prejudices, said I couldn't be a lawyer, and of the publisher who, because she doubted my talent, said I'd never make an editor – ha!) But no. It seems there are as many, if not more, people who will tell you you can't than tell you you can. Sad, isn't it, that there should be so much negative energy floating around? (Imagine if it was turned into positive – what a difference it would make to us as individuals, not to mention society.)

Five Reasons People Will Say You Can't

1 It makes them face up to their own achievements.
People who are happy with their lives and what they have achieved are always enthusiastic about others chasing their dreams as they have nothing to feel threatened by. It reminds me of when someone in an office resigns to take up a position elsewhere. For a while – at least until that person actually leaves – the rest of the office feel unsettled and twitchy about their own positions. I can read it on their faces as they ask themselves 'Should I be leaving? Where is my career going? Perhaps they know something I don't' etc. It's the same in this case: when you propose a change in your life and someone says you can't, what they're actually saying is 'You can't because it makes me uneasy about what I'm doing with my life. Stay as you are, it's comfortable for *me*.'

How to Be Number One in Your Own World

2 They feel affronted that you feel the world in which you both exist isn't good enough.

After all, your desire to change an element of your world can be taken as an expression of dissatisfaction or longing for change. The person who is telling you you can't is often attempting to protect the status quo, and feeling insulted or let down that you don't share their contentment with how things are. I spoke to a woman at a party recently, called Heidi. She was one of the most self-confident, can-do people I've encountered – as a singer in a blues band, you'd think it would go with the territory. But Heidi wasn't always like this. Here's her experience as she told me:

Jeff and I married as soon as we left college. His parents were suc-cessful caterers and, when they retired, they gave Jeff their busi-ness. So I abandoned my plans to pursue a music career and became the wife of a chef. We moved into this nice little suburban house and slowly I turned into this terrible, moody, grey person. I stopped wearing nice clothes and make-up and became a messy housekeeper, never exercised or took care of myself. With each day, I felt worse and worse. But Jeff loved our life – he'd say 'Isn't this great? Our life is wonderful.' He couldn't see it wasn't wonderful for me.

Then I heard that a local band needed a lead singer. I hummed and hawed about whether to call. When I mentioned it to Jeff, he laughed. He said 'You? Come off it, Heid, you can't sing in a band.' Then, one day, I just got the impulse to call for an audi-tion – and I could hardly believe it when I got the job. First we just played in local clubs, then we started to travel further. I final-ly felt happy and energized. Jeff begged me to quit the band and stay home, but for me, the marriage was over. Staying would have killed me. I've realized my dream and have never looked back.

When I asked about her relationship with Jeff now, Heidi said they're not even on speaking terms:

Jeff was so insulted that the life he thought was so wonderful was not wonderful for me and he's never got over it.

3 When someone is genuinely fearful of change, it's difficult for them to contain their fear when confronted with your desire for it.

When they say you can't, what they really mean is 'I can't'. This is often the most dangerous person with whom to share your aspirations because making changes in your life, as well as being exciting and positive, can feel frightening. The change you want to make, after all, is unknown ter-ritory. Being resolute you can is vital when the can't-er attempts to suggest potential obstacles or unpleasant repercussions.

4 Although society is far less prejudiced in the millennium, deep-seated beliefs still prevail.

There are still, for instance, men – and, yes, women – who regard particular attitudes, behaviours or experiences the exclusive right or responsibility of one sex or, indeed, colour or culture. It's unfounded, illogical and, frankly, downright wrong. However, it's worth considering – only for a moment, because that's all it warrants – why they still hold these beliefs.

First, it's a way for the powerful to maintain their power. This is an extreme example, but it doesn't take a genius to work out why men fought for so long against women's right to vote. Until the early 1900s, the male existence was a thoroughly privileged as well as powerful one. While women continued to be denied the vote, this power was protected and unchallenged. These guys were not fools as far as their own wellbeing was concerned, which is why they told women: can't, can't, *can't*!

Second, it's a way for the weak to maintain their weakness. Why would anyone want to exist in a position of weakness? They could be frightened of responsibility, or they may simply feel more comfortable being led or protected from the, sometimes, harsh world. It isn't a wrong way to live (I hope I've stressed already there isn't a wrong or right way to live), but forcing this attitude on someone who craves more power or independence by telling them 'You can't' is certainly narrow-minded and destructive.

5 When someone says 'You can't', perhaps they're simply concerned because of the adjustments they may be forced to make to their own lives.

Let me tell you about Peg, a 35-year-old accountant we featured in an issue of *Cosmo*. She had been a depressed comfort-eater since her teens, and after ten years of marriage, weighed nearly 15 stone. She felt worthless, like she was nothing in her world, never mind number three or four. Finally, although her husband Tim told her she was mad to go for help – 'Peg, you *can't*' – she decided she needed medical advice to get her life on track. So she visited her doctor who recommended some short-term counselling and a diet and exercise programme. She lost a stone and a half right away and began receiving compliments which motivated her to continue with her dream. When she finally attained her goal weight, Peg felt for the first time in her entire life she was controlling her destiny, and she felt happy. But guess what? Her husband, Tim, was grouchy and miserable, even cynical at her achievements. Sneakily, he'd try to woo back his 'old' wife with cakes and pastries and mammoth boxes of chocolates. Peg told us:

I couldn't understand why he wanted me to gain back the weight I'd lost. Eventually, I realized my success was making him anxious and miserable. My sudden surge of self-confidence was a threat to him. Men were starting to pay attention to me, and Tim was jealous – he'd never experienced this before. Finally, he realized I was still me, just more content and that I wasn't going to leave him.

Peg's husband Tim had told her 'you can't', fearful of the repercussions on his life and the changes he might be forced to make to himself. Purely selfish behaviour? Uh-huh. But since Peg's self-esteem has shot up, their marriage is stronger than ever. Make sure you point out to those who say you can't, that the outcome can only be positive – not in spite of the new happier you, but because of the new happier you.

Using Can'ts to Reinforce Your Can

> *Although I believe in myself now, I didn't when I started out. It was a gradual thing. You get fed up with others telling you that you can't and then trying it anyway and finding that you can. I remember when I was a Senior House Officer and pregnant. I kept failing the exams. I remember one occasion when the examiner said to me 'What makes you think you can come here looking like that?' I didn't answer back. I fell apart and failed the exam. When I came out, I felt I had failed myself. And it made me think, 'I'm not going to do that again.'*
>
> **Judy Evans, Plastic Surgeon, Derriford Hospital,**
> **Plymouth**

Do you identify with Judy Evans' experience? Me, too. When I was 24 and told I'd never be an editor, I also remember falling apart. Not for long, mind you. A week later, I began to get angry ... no, let's say *furious*. How dared she? Who the hell was she that she felt she had the right to speak on behalf of the publishing world as well as me and tell me 'You can't – ever'? I realized then that my world, that of publishing, was multi-faceted and comprised many different people and that, okay, she reckoned

I couldn't be an editor of one of her magazines, but, hey, there was a whole world out there who probably had different views on what constituted talent and skill. (Just because you don't like strawberry ice cream doesn't mean strawberry ice cream is bad or sub-standard; it simply means it's not to your taste, but may well be to the taste of someone else, right?)

Without actually realizing what I was doing, I turned her and my own negative energy into positive energy for me. I applied for another editorship. I disregarded her advice, and used all my fury to work harder for this next post than I'd ever worked before. I researched, I planned, I wrote and I read so that by the time the interview came up, I felt invincible. I said to myself 'I can do this. I'm better than she is. I will prove her wrong.'

Guess what? I got that job. It wasn't easy and, between you and me, even seconds before I gave my interview performance, I experienced fleeting doubts. But what got me through was my refusal to be beaten by someone saying 'You can't' for the very thing at that stage in my life I most wanted. My sense of jubilation was overwhelming. I cried the day I got my first editorship, not just through joy because it was what I'd always dreamed of, but because I'd proved my doubter undoubtedly wrong. 'See,' I thought. 'You said I can't. And I've proved I bloody well *can*!'

> *If you think you can, you can. If you think you can't, you can't.*
>
> **Mary Kay Ash, founder of Mary Kay Ash**
> **Mail-order Cosmetics**

So, When Someone Tells You that You Can't …

■ Feel through the fog and try to make contact with why they have said 'You can't'. Is it really a criticism of you, or does it cloak prejudice? Is it based on what they may have experienced before with someone else similar to you? Perhaps if they'd agreed 'You can', it would have left them vulnerable (for instance, 'You can't travel around the Far East, I need you here every day to cook my tea'). It's worth remembering when someone says you can't, this is their opinion only and they are limiting your potential to the boundaries of their world. *Cosmo's* Executive Creative Editor, Leah Hardy, gets over this attitude like this:

When someone tells me you can't, I ask myself whether I want to be like them or live their life. Invariably, the answer is no which makes it easier for me to disregard their opinion and believe I can do whatever it is I want to do.

■ Consider, even only momentarily, why your doubter has said you can't. Beneath the prejudice or unreasonable doubt, there may be small things you can extrapolate to make your journey towards your own aspirations easier. Attempt to separate spite or arrogance or their own insecurity from fact. For instance, they may have said 'You can't ...' due to your lack of experience in a particular area. (For instance, 'You can't be an ice skater, you don't know how to ice skate.') If you don't respect or agree with anything they've said as to why 'You can't ...', don't dwell on it.

■ Imagine your life is a prize and either you are going to win it – or they are. Resolve to make sure you will win by proving them wrong. (I harboured a fantasy that one day, while my 'You can't' publisher was waiting in the rain for a bus, I would drive by in an Aston Martin and spray water in her face. Boy, that fantasy gave me so much impetus, and I used it as a symbol of my prize for winning. Has that fantasy been fulfilled? Well, I did pass her waiting in the pouring rain for a cab, not in my Aston Martin but my Mercedes ... so yes, though it may sound petty, I felt smug in the knowledge I'd won.)

■ Consider the possible outcome if you chose to believe what your doubter says is true. What will probably happen is this: you will give up, stay put, be unhappy, feel miserable, resent people who kick sand in the face of those who say they can't and start using phrases like 'What if ...' and 'If only ...'. Do you really want this for yourself? You wouldn't wish that for anyone else, so of course you don't wish it for yourself. Then consider the possible outcome if you ignore the 'You can't ...'

and go for it and make the dream a reality. How do you feel now? Exhilarated? Relieved? Proud? Happy? Which feelings do you prefer. Quite frankly, there's no contest.

■ Imagine a very good friend of yours is going through your experience and all you want for them is happiness and fulfilment. What would you advise? You would call the person who'd said 'You can't …' all the names under the sun, wouldn't you? You would tell this friend how remarkable they are, how they deserve better treatment than this. You would, quite rightly, be seething with indignation, wouldn't you? I know I would. Write those feelings down or say them out loud. The truth is, most of us are pretty good at bolstering others and making them feel better about themselves and their potential, but dreadful at doing it for ourselves. It's time to treat yourself to a dose of your own medicine.

■ And finally, ask yourself 'Who on earth is this person to say I can't …?' Then remind yourself this person is as human as you or I. She is not God. He does not possess secret powers. He or she is a person with fallibilities who has no doubt made mistakes before and is adding another mistake to their list by claiming 'You can't …'. Accept this is their own personal opinion which you do not happen to share. And now, I'll let you into yet another little trick I use … and let me tell you, it's put many arrogant doubters of my own future into perspective. Here goes: as I've listened to people tell me 'You can't do this/that/the other …', I've imagined them in an undignified situation (my favourite happens to be them straining on the toilet!) and, once I've recovered from my hysterics, it's reminded me these guys are not so powerful or worthy of my devastation after all. Try it, it works – honest!

Give Yourself a Dream Boost – Take a Light Bath

You've made your dream map, you've amassed your tools, so – wonderful – you're halfway to happiness. But all those negative can't-do comments from other people are wearing you down and sapping your can-do confidence. Why not try this practical relaxation exercise called a Light Bath to put your dream back on track. (Warning: sounds a bit new age-y, so don't laugh, just enjoy it for what it is: an indulgence for you and your dream.)

1 Find a quiet place, dim the lights (or turn them off altogether and just light a couple of candles) and lie flat on your back.
2 Focus on your feet and imagine rays of light radiating from your toes.
3 Let them go numb, then imagine the light moving up to your ankles.

4 Imagine you're taking the beams of light up your entire body and out of the top of your head. You should start to feel your body glowing and warm.

5 When you feel as if you're floating, visualize your goal with all its trimmings. You dream of leaving your job and all the responsibilities of debt and mortgages to travel the world? Take yourself there now and imagine yourself boarding the plane, waving to friends and family, settling into your seat and feeling that stomach lurch of excitement as you jet off to faraway lands.

6 Repeat, as they say, when necessary. In other words, each time you need to remind yourself of your ability to fulfil your dream, take a Light Bath and recharge your dream batteries.

CHAPTER 8

Don't Be Frightened, Take Risks

> I believe that anyone can conquer fear by doing the things he fears to do, provided he keeps doing them until he gets a record of successful experiences behind him.
>
> **Eleanor Roosevelt**

When I look back at some of the things I've done in my life, I often think 'Wow! How did I do that? If I knew then what I know now, I'm sure I would never have done that. I would have been too frightened.' I'm sure you feel the same about decisions you've taken in your life. That said, I'm incredibly pleased I didn't know some of the things I know now because I would never have arrived where I am now without taking those risks.

The word 'risk' sounds very grand, the sort of thing only a very brave person takes. In actual fact, risk is only a term for doing something when we don't know what the outcome will be. And unless you can see into the future (and I've yet to come across someone who genuinely can), every day of your life is a risk because you simply don't know what that day will bring.

When you get up in the morning and go to catch your usual bus, you are taking a risk. After all, you don't know whether the bus will break down, take a detour or even be so full you can't get on it in the first place. When you go to work, you don't really know whether you'll be fired or promoted or made redundant. When you visit a restaurant or café for the first time, do you know whether you'll enjoy what you order or whether indeed they'll have anything on the menu you like? It's a risk, isn't it? So why has risk become such a frightening word? Why do we gasp when it's mentioned or utter the word with raised eyebrows and doubtful intonation?

Do you stop queuing for your regular bus because the risk exists that it may break down or be full? Do you stop eating at restaurants because there just may not be anything on the menu that takes your fancy? Of course you don't. You think 'Oh well, I'll give it a go.' And if there really isn't anything on the menu that whets your appetite? It's not the end of the world, is it? You simply get up and leave the restaurant or make the best of your restaurant choice and order a bowl of chips and ketchup and a fabulous pud. No big deal.

So why do you spend so much time thinking about the other risks in your life, the possible outcomes of which may well have more positive meaning in your life than whether you take this bus or visit that restaurant? There are opportunities you could take that could well make you happier and more fulfilled than you are already and lead you towards being number one in your own world.

> *Avoiding danger is no safer in the long run than outright expo-sure. The fearful are caught as often as the bold.*
>
> **Helen Keller**

Why Risks Scare the Life Out of You

Risk. Say the word out loud to yourself. Risk. Risk. RISK. How do you say it? Softly and apprehensively? Loudly and confidently? Do you say it with a smile or with a frown? Do you feel excited or fearful? This simple exercise speaks volumes about the way you view this crucial four-letter word.

But where does your risk perception come from? We're certainly not born with a fear of risk-taking. If we could speak from the day we were born, I guarantee the word risk would not form part of our vocabulary. Let me tell you about something that happened recently (hell, it brings me out in a cold sweat just remembering …). I was visiting a friend who had just moved into an Edwardian house in north London. After she had shown me around, we went downstairs for a coffee, leaving her three-year-old and 18-month-old baby to play in the family room on the first floor. Mid-chat, my friend's three-year-old daughter, Holly, came into the kitchen and began tugging on her

How to Be Number One in Your Own World

arm. 'Mummy ... Mummy ... Mummy ... can I tell you something?' My friend, who is always patient but a stickler for manners, told little Holly, 'Sweetie, just let Mummy finish talking to Mandi and then you can have your say.' Holly didn't seem too bothered so we continued to chat for a couple more minutes. Finally, my friend turned to her daughter who, by now, was drawing flowers and lady-birds at the kitchen table. 'Now, Holly. What did you want to say?' she asked. 'Well, it's just that ...' Holly said, trying to remember what her point was. 'It's just that ... Tom is climbing out of the window.'

Let me tell you the pair of us pelted upstairs like two hungry foxes chasing a rabbit. We screeched to a halt outside the family room and poked our heads around the door. What we saw made us gasp with horror. There was Tom kneeling on the sill of the open window looking at the concrete patio two floors below. 'Christ. Tom ... ' whispered my friend, walking slowly towards her smiling baby, not wanting to frighten him into making any sudden slips. 'Tom, sweetie, stay right there,' she cooed. 'Mummy's here.' As she crept towards Tom, he laughed and looked down. Quick as a flash, my friend lunged towards him, scooped him up and spent the next half an hour kissing and squeezing the daylights out of her non-plussed baby, alternating between telling him off, telling herself off, telling me off and telling him how much she loved him and that she'd die if anything ever happened to him.

This horror story is a great illustration of how risk and fear, unlike smiling and joy, are something we learn rather than something we're born with. For Tom, climbing over the heap of removal boxes and onto the sill was not a risk; it was just a means to experiencing what might be. He was not restricted by the negative possibilities of his actions, but spurred on by the positive possibilities (i.e. that there may have been something fun and exciting over the sill). Since then, Tom hasn't climbed onto the sill. My friend tells me she's caught him eyeing it up a couple of times, but following a strict 'Nooooo' from my friend (who, in any case, will not dare open the window until she gets child guards fitted) has opted against taking the risk. For our own peace of mind, I hope he never does. But, the point is, from a very early age, Tom has learned that there can be unpleasant side-effects from taking risks, and who knows how that will manifest itself in the future?

The other lesson I learned from this, of course, was that my friend was also faced with a risk. The risk was that if she lunged at Tom, he would either scarper off the edge of the sill before she could reach him or she would reach him before he'd had time to move. Fortunately, he stayed put and she was able to scoop him up. But, you know what? It could have gone both ways. As she says 'I would never have forgiven myself if it had gone the other way and I hadn't even tried to grab him.'

Many of the risks we're faced with, thankfully, aren't life-threatening. But it's easy to see how, like Tom, we learn

How to Be Number One in Your Own World

from an early age that there can be negative outcomes from taking a risk (and those negative outcomes are invariably expressed more vehemently than the positive outcomes), so it's best to play safe. But it's also easy to see, isn't it, that playing safe, as in the case of my friend, and not taking the risk (in other words, doing nothing) can be more dangerous.

Ever heard of a man called Ted Turner? Many of you will be too young to remember him, so let me tell you. An American media mogul, Turner was faced with the opportunity of buying the film company, MGM. Yes, it was a huge risk for him. After all, industry experts said he was crazy for buying the struggling empire. But later in life, he often said that the greater risk to him was in *not* buying MGM. Had he not bought MGM, he would not have had the movies necessary for the vast amounts of airtime for his numerous cable channels. Suffice to say, Ted Turner became even wealthier and more successful. But more than that, he became *the* number one in his world.

As we grow from baby to toddler, through to tot, then child, then teenager, it seems the negative aspects of risk-taking prevail over the positive. We are encouraged to believe that only if we conform to the rules of others will we be 'good'. Most of us are told by our parents and teachers that if we break rules, take chances, try and discover things for ourselves, the most likely outcome is misery, regret, heartbreak, failure.

Which is why so often when we reach adulthood and are faced with taking risks to try and improve our lives, seek out more happiness and fulfilment, create our own world, we decide not to take the risk. To play it safe. To avoid the possibility of the risk going both ways, by sticking to what we know, even if what we know isn't making us happy.

> *What the hell — you might be right, you might be wrong — but don't just avoid.*
>
> **Katharine Hepburn**

A reader wrote into *Cosmo* not so long ago asking advice about her relationship. She told us she was in a long-term relationship with a man she believed loved her, but who (not often, just sometimes) punched her. This man was adored by all her friends and family. After all, he was fun and generous and hard-working. She confided in a friend who, she discovered, was experiencing the same kind of relationship, but this friend advised her to stay put, saying: 'After all, better the devil you know than the devil you don't'.

How, I asked myself after reading this letter, could anyone with her friend's happiness and wellbeing at heart give such advice? How did she know that her friend would never find a better man, a man who wouldn't even 'just sometimes' punch her? Could any man be worse? Conversely, there's a jolly good chance that another man could be better, so much better. The probabilities are very very high.

What's more, even if she never found another partner, could it be any worse than being in a relationship that was violent? And anyway, as this reader confided, she was no longer happy in this relationship. She felt undermined; her confidence was ebbing away; she was beginning to mistrust her judgement. It doesn't take a degree in psychology to work out she was at greater risk of remaining unhappy by staying – by not doing anything – than leaving.

The problem is that, without realizing it, most of us live according to a set of rules which, although unwritten, control our behaviour. These rules are drummed into us from school and from our earliest years at home, listening to our parents, watching television, reading books and newspapers. They are very old rules and do not allow for the needs and desires and dreams of the individual, their sole purpose being to maintain the status quo. One rule is 'Stay at the same company, work hard and you will be the boss and be happy' (the inference being that if you don't, you'll spend your life in abject poverty and misery). Another rule is 'Find a partner, fall in love, buy a house, have children and you'll be happy and secure' (again, the inference being, if you do not, you will be alone and desolate).

Although so much has changed in our society since the turn of the 1900s, many of the rules we (particularly women) still live by are derived from that age. Taking risks does not enter the picture. In fact, we're taught risk-taking is a sure ticket to hell, kicking, as it does, sand in the face of all these rules. Women, particularly, can find taking risks uncomfortable for two reasons: biology and sociology. Women naturally have lower levels than men of testosterone, the hormone that drives us to take risks, as well as being responsible for aggression, competitiveness and a high sex drive. Combined with the historical 'training' of women to revere security (of the household and children) rather than risk, it's hardly surprising many of us put our dreams on the backburner to allow the happiness of others to boil over. Which is why our reader felt so distraught she was compelled to write to *Cosmo*. Fortunately, we were able to point out to her that risk can be a very positive thing – there's always at least a 50 per cent chance that the outcome will be great. We were also able to point out that in her case not acting or taking the appropriate risk could be more dangerous than taking it. In the context of this book, moreover, not taking the risk was ensuring her sociable, hard-working yet violent boyfriend was number one in her world, not her, because she was giving in to his comfort at the expense of her own.

I think that's precisely what growing up is – steadily learning to take more and greater risks. While it's easy – and helpful – to see the facility for risk-taking grow in a child, it's important to remember that this process continues all our lives.

Gloria Steinem, social reformer
Quote from interview in *Cosmopolitan* (1989)

Change Your Approach to Risk

There's no getting away from it – being number one in your own world requires taking risks. There's a pretty good chance you will need to make some changes in your life or perhaps act out of character (or what others perceive your character to be). You may have to inconvenience some who have come to rely upon you. But, think of it this way: in most cases, risk-taking is invigorating and exciting. Think of a fairground: the most exciting ride is the roller coaster which appears a damn sight riskier than the carousel but isn't. Okay, so it may make you feel frightened but, hey, how exhilarated do you feel when you've experienced the ride? What's more, once you've ridden the roller coaster, it doesn't seem quite so risky, does it? You feel more confident about taking a ride for a second time, maybe a third. However, if you never take the first ride, that huge roller coaster seems very intimidating and risky from where you're standing, down below on the safe, solid, boring ground where little ever happens.

A lack of self-confidence is what holds many of us back from pursuing our dreams and being number one in our worlds. Yet confidence is built on taking risks and overcoming our fear of the unknown. Of all the people I've interviewed and chatted to for this book, what I've realized is that those who really are number one in their own worlds don't regard risks as austere, intimidating, closed doors to be bashed in with a sledgehammer, thereby breaking your arm in the process and leaving you wrung out, tired and miserable with the fight. They regard risks as welcoming, open doors that symbolize positive opportunities to pursue their dreams. They talk of becoming stronger with every risk they take and every milestone conquered, and they become stronger, wiser and more prepared for the next risk or challenge.

For instance, PR guru and author, Lynne Franks, told me of the risk she took, aged just 21, when she dreamed of starting up her own PR company:

I really believed in it, that it was right for me. So I left a safe job and also turned down another very good job that would have been exciting and lucrative. It was a huge risk, but once I had taken the leap and was actually doing it, it wasn't so daunting.

If she hadn't taken what to many of her peers and older colleagues was regarded as a crazy risk, Lynne Franks may well have been a successful PR guru anyway. But would she have been truly fulfilled and happy? Would she have been number one in her world?

I'm also thinking of another of the last century's icons, the passive and seemingly docile Mother Teresa (who, sadly, I was never able to interview). She defied the experts in her desire and dream to help the poor. She broke the rules of her order, asking the Pope for permission to leave her order and live in the ghettos of Calcutta. This was not only unprecedented but an enormous personal risk as well. But she was able to gain Papal approval, and lived and worked among the leper colonies for 50 years, defying medical science. Mother Teresa, however, never considered this as a risk, but as an opportunity to use her position of power to make extraordinary gains. Her success earned her a Nobel Prize.

Don't Let Your 'Limitations' Stop You Taking Opportunities

When you substitute the word 'opportunity' for 'risk', the future does not seem so scary. The unknown becomes thrilling and bright rather than peppered with mines and the potential for failure. The word 'opportunity' forces you to consider and believe in your strengths and the wonderful possibility of unknown achievements. The word 'risk' brings you face to face with your vulnerabilities and weaknesses … in other words, what you think of as your limitations.

And it's our obsession with our limitations that stops us taking risks. Wallowing around in our limitations is a habit that's hard to shake. I know this. After all, when we leave school, most of us do so with qualifications we're expected to show to the world that *prove* our limitations. If we don't achieve a good A-level grade in art, say, we believe we're not very creative. If we only achieve a 'C' in maths, we believe we're only average at maths. If we have no qualifications at all, we take it that we're not very bright and, therefore, able to do very little.

Philosopher, Deepak Chopra, believes we tend to limit our potential opportunities in life based on our idea of what 'is' rather than what 'can be' and I agree with him. You'll agree with him too if you've ever thought 'Based on what I know, I can/can't do X or Y'. In other words, too much knowledge is a bad thing. You doubt it? Listen to this story recorded by medical science:

Eight men were trapped in a cave and knew they would die unless they were rescued within days because of their lack of food and water. Only one man had a watch, so he was assigned the responsibility for announcing the elapsed time to the others so they would know their chances of living. The man lied to keep up the spirits of the others. He told them 30 minutes had elapsed when an hour had gone by. He kept up this fabrication for days. The group was rescued a week later, far too long for any them to have lived without water. Everyone was alive except the time-keeper, who knew the truth. Too much knowledge had killed him, while too little knowledge had saved the others!

What a great tale. *Now* do you doubt it?

When I interviewed Anita Roddick, founder of The Body Shop, for this book, she gave me an on-the-ground illustration of her own experience of the theory that knowing your limitations can hold you back from achieving your dreams:

When I came back from travelling where I'd lived in fishing and small agricultural communities, I dreamed of setting up a beauty business that adhered to a philosophy of social responsibility — using natural cocoa butter to rub on your body or pineapple to clean your skin. But I had no idea how to shape my idea. There were no business schools then and I didn't know anything about economic theories so I didn't know what I couldn't do. If we had been aware of what we couldn't do, or shouldn't do, I'm sure we would never have had the confidence to develop The Body Shop into the business it is today.

None of us has limitations. The only limitations we have are those we *think* we have, whether we have been told of those limitations by others or imposed them on ourselves. This means that very little is beyond our capability. Let me tell you quickly about a risk I faced head-on recently that challenged my perception of my limitations. I received a phone call inviting me on to the panel of the news and current affairs programme *Question Time*. I confess, when I discussed it with the head of our communications department, I bleated 'No, I can't. I know my limits.' Looking back, I feel very silly indeed, but at the time, the risk that I would make a complete banana of myself by attempting to even discuss politics among politicians and news commentators was just too hideous to contemplate. I had nightmares that I would appear on the programme and completely forget even the name of the prime minister, thereby rendering me a laughing stock which would then result in me either being fired from my job or being forced to resign out of shame.

After weeks of sleepless nights and days of boring friends and colleagues rigid with my self-doubt, I decided to take the risk, even if my motive was that I'd be damned if any other magazine editor was going to appear on the programme instead of me. As the filming drew nearer and panic turned to hysteria, I decided to take action. The only way I was going to minimize the risk of public humiliation and defeat was to absorb myself in a crash course in world politics. By the day of the show, there wasn't a single thing I didn't know about Kosovo, Saddam Hussein, the IRA or the government's policy on teenage mothers.

I'd be lying if I told you that, despite all the preparation, I breezed on to *Question Time* without a second's stomach clench. On the contrary, I could hear my heart pounding in my ears and my palms were as soggy as two little sponges. But I got through the show. I even earned a couple of rounds of applause so that by the time the credits rolled, I was as high as a kite and wondering what all the fuss was about. What I had thought was my limit clearly wasn't. I hadn't appeared foolish or thick. In fact, I'd done the magazine and my employers proud. Most importantly, I'd done myself proud by proving to myself I had no limit and that what I thought was a risk was actually a wonderful opportunity to reveal a different dimension of myself to the public, to my friends, family, employers — and to me.

So next time you find yourself asking 'Can I take the risk?', be sure you remind yourself there is nothing to stop you. Then change the question to 'Can I take the opportunity?' and shout 'Yes!'. I know I certainly will.

When I went to university, I discovered there were two sets of people: those who worked really hard and those who were naturally brilliant. I was one of those who worked hard, but all the same it was daunting and a struggle. Because I loved writing and knew I wanted to write for a living when I left university, I decided I'd start with the university magazine. But it took me until my second year to realize the people who got ahead were the ones who pushed to the front of the queue and demanded. So in my first year, I was weasly old listings editor, which was sad. But in my second year, I forced my way into becoming arts editor. It was a risk and, although I was a good writer, I was an absolutely terrible arts editor. This is an example of just how bad I was — someone wrote a review of a classical concert and I edited out the name of the conductor! But the point is I was still able to put that I was arts editor of Cambridge University's magazine on my CV, which I know set me apart from the competition when I started job-hunting. There's little point being a good writer if you don't have the confidence to push to the front of the queue when opportunities present themselves.

**Anna Maxted, novelist and *Cosmopolitan*
contributing editor**

It's Great to Take Risks/Opportunities Because ...

- ... there's at least a 50 per cent chance the outcome will be positive.
- ... if you're unhappy or dissatisfied or unfulfilled now, the outcome can *only* be positive.
- ... there is no limit to what you can do.
- ... with every risk you take, you become stronger, wiser, more confident.
- ... every risk you take brings you nearer to being number one in your world.

Risk-taking is the cornerstone of empires.

Estée Lauder

How to Be Number One in Your Own World

CHAPTER 9

Don't Even Consider Failure

> *Failure? The possibilities do not exist.*
>
> **Margaret Thatcher**

When we worry about failure, what's happening is that we are really admitting to a lapse or shortage of self-confidence. When we worry that a relationship may fail, few of us consider the possibility that we'll go off our partners, but that they will go off us. When we are nervous about a job interview, we rarely worry we won't like the interviewer, but that they will not like us. When we are anxious that a business we've set up could fail, we don't consider the malfunction of our computers or stock, but that we may make huge gaffs or oversights. And when we predict we'll fail in our dreams, we do so because we suspect we aren't strong/quick/smart/sexy/witty enough.

Fear of failing or lack of self-confidence is the single biggest obstacle to becoming number one in your own world. For starters, it impacts on your physical health in astonishing ways. It makes your shoulders slump and your walk unsteady. It's what causes you to avert your eyes, scratch your nose, twiddle your hair, poke your ears. It brings on eczema, upset stomachs, pimple-breakouts, dry mouths and shortage of breath.

Fear of failing also affects how we live from day to day. It stops you striding into a shop and demanding your money back on faulty goods ('They'll say no') and stops you inviting people out to lunch ('They won't want to have lunch with me'). It inhibits your contribution in meetings, at parties, over dinner, in bed ('I'll look foolish'). It prevents you from sticking two fingers up at people who take advantage of your generosity or easy-going nature ('I'll lose my friends'). And it prevents you from buying the sorts of fashionable clothes you covet from the pages of magazines ('They won't suit me'), experimenting with different hairstyles ('I'll look ridiculous'), changing your route to work ('I'll probably be late'), approaching potential friends and lovers ('I'm not loveable'), taking cello or driving or pottery lessons ('I'll fail').

Even worse, it stops dreams dead in their tracks.

From the quietest to the cleverest, the wittiest and loudest, fear of failure and lack of self-confidence are what almost everyone suffers from in their life. But it's the degree to which you allow them to rule your life that I'm most interested in. Because even the tiniest lapse of self-confidence can have catastrophic effects in the pursuit of your dreams. Sounds extreme? Not if you consider that it only takes one phone call never made because you felt inadequate, one person ignored because you didn't feel you were desirable/loveable/employable, one decision never

How to Be Number One in Your Own World

taken because you felt you didn't have the right to follow your heart or beliefs, one letter never sent because you feared the competition was so much better than you.

Think about the times you have felt most confident. Wouldn't it be great if you could bottle that feeling? Personally, I always feel my most confident after I've been on holiday, when I've had time to think and I'm feeling relaxed and full of holiday glow. And it's often following a holiday that I've felt confident enough to take decisions that have had the most significant effect on my life.

I remember one instance as if it were yesterday. I had just returned from a cheap holiday in Turkey with a close girlfriend, during which we'd sunned ourselves, danced till dawn and dreamed the days away. We'd asked ourselves the sorts of questions, lying there on the beach, you never normally have the time to consider, such as 'What would really make you happy?', 'What's the one thing you would change about your life right now if you could?'.

On my return to the office a week later, I received a phone call from a former colleague. As I was too busy catching up with work to take the call, my assistant took her message. The next day, I came across the message and, for a fleeting moment, asked myself whether I should return her call – I had, after all, not been that close to her. But as I was still in my holiday never-say-no-to-anything mood, I decided 'What the hell?' and returned her call. She told me about the editorship of a magazine going in the company where she was working and, although she wasn't sure if the position had been filled, she felt I would be perfect for that job.

Although I was fantastically excited about the prospect of this particular magazine, for a fleeting moment I wondered whether it was worth me applying; after all, it was a much bigger job than I was used to in a company that had always seemed far too glamorous for me. And anyway, I thought, I'm sure lots of brilliant people will apply so I won't stand a cat in hell's chance. So I put the details to one side and carried on catching up with my job. But as I wandered around the West End during my lunch, I remembered the conversations I'd had on holiday. When my friend had asked 'What's the one thing you would change about your life right now if you could?', I had answered with a sigh 'To be the editor of a "grown-up" magazine where I would be taken seriously and my abilities recognized.' So why was I procrastinating? Why wasn't I leaping at the chance to make my dream a reality? Had I not been clinging to that holiday confidence, I might very well *never* have charged back to the office and rattled out the most outrageous, exuberant, yes, arrogant, letter of my life. I might very well have concluded that, no, I wasn't bright or experienced or talented enough to even be considered, never mind get through an inevitably tough first interview. My fear of failure, frankly, wouldn't have given success a chance.

Within two hours of hand-delivering my application, however, the managing director of this publishing company, was on the phone inviting me for an interview that evening. Once again, in normal circumstances, I might well have had second thoughts. Hell, I wasn't in the least bit prepared for this and if you had seen what I was wearing ... shorts and T-shirt, hardly a regular interview outfit. But, well, my frame of mind was such I felt I could fly, walk on water. Ha! Today I felt like a genius, a magazine tiger, a publishing queen! Fail? Are you kidding? I felt so confident, there was nothing I couldn't succeed at ... even if I *was* wearing tatty shorts and a T-shirt.

And you know what? I'm convinced that it wasn't what I said in that interview that eventually won me the job I wanted, but *how* I said it – with conviction, with fire, with absolute confidence. I knew I glowed with it. And that confidence made me smile, stand tall, throw my voice so that the passion became contagious. Because I appeared so confident in me, my prospective employer had confidence in me. And, beyond my wildest dreams, I was offered the job as Editor of *Company* magazine, my first big editing job and the springboard to Editor-in-Chief of *Cosmopolitan*.

Since then, my confidence has grown. That's the beauty of confidence: once you've realized the power of it, it makes you more confident still. And it grows ... and grows ... and grows. Sure, you have knocks along the way, that's life. But you're never quite knocked back to how you felt before you discovered the power of the big C.

Where Your Fear of Failure Comes From

We know that babies aren't born with a lack of confidence and a fear of failure. Every young child I know will stand up and sing at the top of her voice a couple of verses of 'Twinkle, twinkle, little star', given half the chance. They're immune to their audience's chortles when they hit a duff note or muddle their words. And, at the drop of a hat, any child will take part in a race to the bottom of the garden and back ... even if they can't yet walk, they'll have a go by crawling. No fear of failure there. No sense of humiliation if they don't win, just pure joy and exhilaration that they've joined in the race and had fun.

So what happens? If we really look back at our lives, most of us can recall a couple of instances that have had an enormous and long-lasting impact on our self-confidence. Maybe it was the environment in which you were brought up. Were you always put down as a child? Do you have a painful memory of being laughed at or scorned that has made you reluctant to ever put yourself in the spotlight again? Perhaps it was more subtle than that – a kind of drip-drip-drip erosion of your confidence that resulted in you believing that, regardless of what you did, you were doomed to fail?

A friend of mine, a successful freelance writer, says her lack of confidence comes from her childhood attempts at gaining the attention of her father, a distant and cold man:

It didn't matter what I did, he never praised me or showed me affection. In the end, I realized it didn't matter what I did, I wasn't going to be successful in gaining his admiration or respect. As a consequence, I grew up believing that whatever I did, however hard I tried, it would never be enough. It's been very difficult recovering that loss of self-esteem.

Perhaps one or both of your parents, or indeed teachers, lacked confidence in themselves, which instilled in you a dangerous attitude of 'Don't try, you'll only fail'. Another friend, Emma, now a department store merchandiser, recalls her mother's response the day she auditioned for a part in her school play:

We were working on a production of Toad of Toad Hall. *I fancied myself as the lead, Toady, and had rehearsed the lines for weeks. I asked my mother if I could practise in front of her. Halfway through, she burst out laughing. When I asked her why she was laughing, she said 'Why are you going for this? You'll only make a fool of yourself.' I was so upset. I still went for the part, but in the back of my mind I could hear my mother reminding me I'd be humiliated. I didn't get the part, of course. I was terrible, I know it. And although I'd love to act or do something in the theatre, even if it's only amateur dramatics, I still couldn't get up on a stage even now for fear I'd be a failure. The thing is, I know my mother would have loved to act — in fact, she's got a great voice. But because she never had the chance, she didn't want me to have the chance either and she destroyed my confidence to even try.*

Mary, a friend of a friend, now a Human Resources Manager for a big city firm, says her mother wasn't so obviously dismissive of her abilities but damaged her confidence nevertheless:

My mother had grown up believing marriage and kids were everything she should want so she wasn't particularly confident in her approach to the outside world. In the week of my GCSEs, I told her I was worried about some of my subjects. Instead of telling me to just give it my best, she said she'd never done anything if she thought she was going to fail. As a result, I only sat three exams. I passed them with flying colours and I'm sure I wasn't half as bad at the other subjects as I'd thought I was. I later sat those exams and passed no problem. But I have had to fight my lack of confidence all the way as I was brought up to believe you should give in to your doubts and fear of failure. Trouble is, succumbing to your lack of confidence doesn't make you feel more confident about what you can do, it makes you less confident, so you stop trying to do anything.

Your Self-confidence – the Key to Being Number One

Take a look at the people whose position of being number one in their own worlds you admire. Let me throw a few names into the hat for consideration: Oprah Winfrey? The Spice Girls? Madonna? Golda Meir? Margaret Thatcher? Why these people succeeded in their own worlds was down to their self-confidence. Oprah Winfrey didn't have a Masters in psychology but confesses she believed she was special. (As a little child, she announced she would be 'paid to talk' when she became an adult.) Within six months of starting out, she overtook daytime TV king Phil Donohue by surpassing his ratings, going on to become the most famous and respected pop psychologist in the world.

Ex-Spice Girl, Geri Halliwell, like the other Spices, struggled for years to achieve her celebrity dream. Did she get there through exceptional talent? We don't think so. She got there through sheer outrageous self-promotion and self-confidence. Likewise Madonna. She was talented yes, but so were a million other singing wannabes. What set Madonna apart was (in the words of a record company president), 'When she walked into the room, she filled it with her exuberance and determination.' She never once gave in to the possibility of failure. And because she didn't, those around her were not confronted with the possibility either. It's thanks to Madonna's utter self-confidence rather than her musical skill that she has broken the rules and boundaries in music and become the wealthiest woman in the industry.

Golda Meir, who defied a male-dominated electorate and made it to the top of an Israeli government where she was prime minister for five years, described herself as having 'more than my fair share of self-confidence'. Not unlike Margaret Thatcher, who was the longest-serving prime minister of the 20th century. I laughed out loud when I read of her retort when told by a school teacher that she was lucky to have won a debating contest. 'I was not lucky,' she said. 'I deserved it.' It was this mega-dose of self-belief and denial of the possibility of failure, which not only contributed to Thatcher becoming Prime Minister of Great Britain, but kept her there undaunted for 11 years.

None of the above examples of huge success in their own worlds had much to do with exceptional intelligence or gargantuan IQs. Neither did they have privileged backgrounds to give them a leg up. Succeeding at being number one in your own world is about something more basic than anything you could see written on paper. It's all about self-confidence and belief in yourself. It's about having a dream and believing that you – and only you – are capable of making it happen. Failure will only creep into the equation if *you* don't have the confidence to keep it out.

Take the Fear of Failure Out of Your Life

Society is preoccupied with winning rather than doing. This makes us feel, from our earliest days, that if we don't come first in a race or beat everyone in the class at history, we're a failure in that activity and open to ridicule or pity or the feeling that our efforts were simply worthless. It's hardly surprising, then, based on this criteria, that over the years our self-confidence is put under the hammer, day after day. It's a wonder any of us reach adulthood with a shred of self-confidence left intact.

So how can you change your perception of failure – and banish it for good?

Don't confuse other people's idea of failure with your own. The definition of failure is purely subjective. The truth is, if you don't come first in a race, it simply means that at that moment among that particular group of people, you didn't run as fast as those who finished before you. It doesn't mean you're a hopeless athlete. This was one isolated incident with a benchmark of success determined by one person. So ya boo sucks! To one person, the fact you didn't finish first in a race may constitute failure. It would be a short-sighted definition, but it is, nevertheless, their definition and they're entitled to it. Ensure your definition is much more positive. Okay, you may have finished last in the race that stretches 1500 metres, but if previously you have only been able to run 100 metres, the fact you have completed 1500 metres is an amazing success for you. And I stress *for you* because it is you that matters. We are talking about successes in your own world, not in the world of other people.

Be confident in your efforts.
No one has ever accomplished anything that really matters to them simply through luck or skill. It always requires an element of self-confidence. Psychologists have found time and again that those who think positively tend to perform positively and those who think negatively usually perform negatively. If you ski you'll know what I'm saying here. Thinking positively about skiing down a difficult slope conditions your muscles positively and ensures a high probability of success. On the other hand, if you think negatively, your body becomes stiff and your muscles taut, which virtually guarantees you'll fall ... just as you believed you would. The greatest athletes never allow their minds to get in the way of their bodies. Don't allow your mind to get in the way of your dreams.

Banish failure from your vocabulary.
If there is only one possible outcome – success – then the outcome of what you do will be positive. I know this sounds naive, but it *does* take into account obstacles along

the way, believe me. The key is not to regard any outcome you didn't want to experience as failure. Think of it merely as something you will need to side-step to reach your ultimate positive goal. When a close friend of mine, Jane, had a dream of changing career and becoming a make-up artist, she completed a college course and embarked on a series of interviews with agencies. After her first disappointing interview, she could have said 'I failed'. Instead, she regarded it as the successful completion of one interview, took advice from the agency booker, collected a few more tear sheets of her artistic work and marched off to the next interview, feeling more confident and sure of success. She was signed up. Since then, there have been occasions when photographic shoots haven't always gone the way she would like. But they have been isolated incidents that have empowered her with more knowledge and experience to ensure she never has to endure a repeat performance.

Understand that your best is a huge success.
Thinking only about winning is actually counter-productive, in many cases, to winning. Ego gets in the way of performance. Winning becomes the only criteria for success rather than great individual performance. If you use 'the best you can possibly be' as the criteria for your success, you can't fail as long as you actually are the best you can possibly be. Don't measure yourself against other people.

Their achievements have nothing to do with your achievements. Create your own targets. Set your own goals. Define your own terms of success. Being number one in your own world is about identifying your own skills and styles and then capitalizing on them as best as you can. That is true success.

How to Be Number One in Your Own World

CHAPTER 10

Dealing with Setbacks

Not a single success story would be complete – or true – without mention of setbacks. Why? Simple. Because, although it would be nice, you're not always in control of other people's responses or actions. (Unfortunately, neither are you at times entirely in control of your health or safety.) If setbacks weren't a natural part of life, there would be no need for this book. We would all have our dreams aged, say, seven or eight and have achieved them by the time we were, well, nine! And think how dull life would be. If everything happened for us so easily, there would actually be no such thing as dreams. There would be no need for courage, creativity, wit or sense. Neither would there be excitement, anticipation, relief or exhilaration ... all those emotions that propel us out of bed each morning and fill us with joy when we experience them.

Believe it or not, setbacks are the very things that make us great. They test our resilience and knowledge; they push our creativity and inventiveness to levels we never thought possible; they arm us with more information than we had before we encountered them, increasing our skill and boosting our brain power; they force us to be stronger physically and emotionally to enable us to cope when we finally arrive at our destination (that destination, of course, Number One, Own World). Setbacks are the very crossroads of our success, forcing us to appreciate how far we've come and allowing us to genuinely congratulate ourselves for our achievements.

A setback in itself is not truly a setback. It's how you handle it that makes it a setback — or not. When I was in my early 20s and hungry for a writing job on a magazine, I applied for every job in Monday's *Media Guardian*. A fortnight later, the rejection letters would roll in. Were they setbacks? Well, in truth, I regarded them as hideous setbacks at the time. And I'd wallow around in self-pity and misery for days. But they weren't *really* setbacks — I, unwittingly at the time, didn't allow them to be setbacks to my success. Seventy-two hours later I'd find myself fired up and back at the keyboard, determinedly rattling off a different article that gave my portfolio of cuttings an extra dimension which eventually landed me a job I loved and paved the way for future successes.

Overcoming setbacks is rather like experiencing heartbreak. The first time you really have your heart broken in two, you feel (no, you *vow*) you'll never get over it. It physically hurts. You feel desolate. And it takes weeks, sometimes months, even years, to feel normal again. But you do. And are subsequent heartbreaks ever so painful? Rarely, if not never. That's because each time after the

How to Be Number One in Your Own World

first, you know that, although you'll cry and hurt and look like an utter wreck for ages after, you will learn to live – and laugh – again. From that first painful experience you will have learned certain mechanisms to make yourself feel better. You might have learned who your real friends are, those you can truly rely on. You may also have learned characteristics about yourself that you will be mindful of in the future. You will most certainly have learned about the characteristics you need to avoid in future partners. That first heartbreak is only a setback to finally discovering true love if you either never allow yourself to heal or if, once healed and enjoying life again, you hook up with an identical partner with whom you behave in an identical fashion.

Thinking Positively about Setbacks

Urgh! *Setback*. What a revolting word. It's even more revolting when you dissect it. Think about it: set means stuck and back means past. So how do you fancy being stuck in the past? No thank you. What? Never to enjoy fresh and different experiences? Never to learn anything new? Never to move forwards or upwards and to experience the exhilaration and thrill of doing so? Aaagh! Kill me now! And take you with me. Is that really what you want? Always being stuck back in number three or four slot in your own world, while everyone else gets on and enjoys life? No, no, no.

You can overcome anything. Nothing, absolutely nothing, is insurmountable. So let's not talk about setbacks. Let's add that ugly little word to our list of unrepeatables. Because once it ceases to exist in our vocabulary, it ceases to exist as a possibility. Let's talk instead of obstacles, yes, such as mountains, hurdles, boulders, gaps, canyons, because becoming number one in your own world is all about striding forwards, climbing upwards, leapfrogging obstacles, skimming around boulders, knocking over hurdles, scaling mountains. All these things can be difficult, of course, but impossible? No.

Do you think my opinions are naive? If you do, perhaps you are naive. If you truly believe there are some obstacles that can't be overcome, you need to get to know more people who have succeeded in being number one in their world. Listen, let me tell you about two young women I met some months ago at a glittering, yet humbling, *Cosmopolitan* breakfast to celebrate our Women of Achievement Awards. The first true tale I'll tell you regards a shy yet ferociously determined then 28-year-old freelance film director called Minkie Spiro who won our Creative Arts Award. This is what she told me:

I started as a photographer, then I wanted to use words with my images. I wanted to tell stories, real stories. So I finished my first degree in photography at Central Saint Martin's and applied to New York University to do a course in film directing. I didn't get in and was dreadfully disappointed. In fact, I felt so crushed, my

How to Be Number One in Your Own World

sister almost had to bully me to apply instead for an MA in film directing at the Royal College of Art. I don't know how I got on that course as I didn't have the right experience, and the competition was tough, but I was accepted. Six months into my MA, however, I had a brush with death. Since then, I've spent several years in and out of hospital recovering. At one point, after days of feeling unwell, I had a heart attack from all the medicines the doctor gave me and ended up in a coma.

When I eventually came around, I went through a denial period. Then came the shock and trauma, then self-pity. I thought, 'Why me?'. And then I experienced terrible grief. I was completely paralysed at one point. Even now I walk with a stick. But I feel as though I was given a second chance. According to the doctors, I wasn't going to survive. If you'd told me two years ago that I would be walking with a stick, I would have been devastated. But often we learn the hard way.

Somehow, I managed to complete my MA while still undergoing treatment. Then I had the opportunity of pitching for a film commission for the BBC. I was only two weeks out of hospital and when I went for the interview I could only whisper as my vocal cords were very weak. I also had problems with my eyes so I had to wear sunglasses – I looked ridiculous. But I wasn't going to let my ill health get the better of me, and out of 1000 people who applied, I was one of the ten who won a commission. The film I made – Rat Women – ended up doing so well it fronted the series, which is the highest form of flattery you can get as the first film provides the publicity for the rest of the series.

When I fell ill, I thought it was the worst thing that could have possibly happened to me — now I realize I needed it to happen. I learned from it. It's more like enlightenment and the realization that enlightenment doesn't necessarily mean switching on the light, but seeing in the dark. The paths of your life or your career can never be etched in stone. You've got to go with the flow. You have to see beyond the negative or traumatic. You have to be open and flexible. And if you don't get something, you have to remember, your time will come — if not then, another time. You'll be successful somewhere else, or in something else. You must never be too devastated by disappointments — there is always good in all the bad.

Now do you think I'm naive? Now can you think of a single obstacle that can't be overcome? Let me tell you about another amazing woman I met that morning at *Cosmopolitan's* Women of Achievement Awards. Her name is Merlyn Nuttall, now 34 (1999), and she went on not only to win her Voluntary category, but scooped the overall Woman of Achievement Award. This is why:

One morning, Merlyn, then just 26, and a successful fashion buyer for a nationwide department store, was attacked on her way to work. Her assailant dragged her into a derelict house where he raped, garrotted and set fire to her, then left her for dead in the burning house. Miraculously, she escaped and survived, after 400 stitches in her neck.

After recovering, she was determined to help police convict the man who almost killed her and, 11 months later, he was jailed for 33 years. Discovering a desperate shortage of counselling literature for people like her, Merlyn wrote a book entitled *It Could Have Been You* to help other survivors. Now she campaigns for fair treatment of rape victims and, while fighting to rebuild her own life, works tirelessly in a voluntary capacity for victim support. She even helped to launch the first Victim Support helpline. What's more, the trauma Merlyn experienced made her even more determined to fulfil her dream — to own and run her own fashion business. She told me:

Because my attack was so life-threatening, I felt very lucky to be alive. There were three times during the attack when I truly thought I was going to die. As a result, I view my life now as extra time and I'm not prepared to waste a minute of it. Even though I knew I couldn't change what had happened to me in the past, I knew I could change my attitude for the future, to make sure it was a happy life in front of me. I could have felt bitter, but bitterness would have only harmed me more and I didn't want my attacker to ruin the rest of my life. It was that thought which has been a spur for me to ensure I overcame any feelings of hatred I had for him. In fact, I never had to cross that barrier because I always focused on the future.

Merlyn didn't even consider making her dream a reality until five years after her attack. It took her years to rebuild her confidence and independence and come to terms with her experience. It was a gradual process of learning to cope with the experiences so many of us take for granted, such as just walking down a street or travelling on our own. As Merlyn said to me:

The one thing trauma takes away is the feeling of control you have over your life. You don't realize this until it happens to you. So the one thing I wanted back was that control. I had to start with simple tasks and I made a checklist of what I wanted to do, such as travel, such as be independent. But then two years ago, I decided the time was right to really get my life back and move forward. I always felt it was my destiny to have my own fashion business, but you know what? I don't know how quickly it would have happened if the attack hadn't taken place. These days, I know life is too short to waste time.

Today, Merlyn owns and runs her own fashion business, Frockbrokers (a cross between a designer shop and dress agency), in partnership with her boyfriend, Andrew:

I love it. Before the attack, I always had this worry about taking risks. That life was like a game of snakes and ladders in that you could make a move but if you slipped you could end up being worse off than where you were. But I know now that you just have to try everything. I also know you can't live your life in the shadow of a trauma. Live the future optimistically; don't let one or two incidents, however big or small, ruin the rest of your life. Life is too precious.

Don't Hit Obstacles – Jump Them!

Question: if we now accept that obstacles can occur to hinder our attempts at being number one in our own world, aren't we considering failure? And if we consider failure to be a possibility, aren't we contradicting what we've learned from the previous chapters?

Answer: definitely no.

Those who have achieved the enviable status of number one (in their own world) have accepted that there could well be obstacles, but have never lost the belief that they will nevertheless succeed in their overall objective. Dreamers, yes, but realists, too, which has resulted in a fighting spirit that doesn't allow them to be defeated at the first hurdle. On the contrary, they have become more determined dreamers knowing they will have to scale mountains and thrash through oceans, but that it will be worth it when they arrive at their destination.

So how do you prepare for obstacles without allowing them to dilute your passion for that number one slot in your own world? Here are some tricks I've learned along the way, and some even better ones I've picked up from others who have been generous enough to share them with me:

Trick 1: Walk up to your obstacle
First, write down – or say out loud – the worst thing that could happen en route to your dream. Now write down

what you would do if that worst case scenario became reality. Having walked up to your worst fear and made a plan for its eventuality, the possibility suddenly seems less intimidating. You can now get on with pursuing your dream without the worry of 'what if's' hanging over your head and chipping away at your energy levels as well as confidence. What's more, should your worst fear come true, you're prepared and ready to strike, having already, calmly and logically, planned your response or alternative route to success.

Trick 2: Draw an A–Z to your dream

Most of you, if you live in a city, will possess an A–Z road map. Living in London, mine is particularly dog-eared – there are always infuriating roadworks and overnight appearances of 'No Entry' signs that prevent me getting to where I need to be and necessitate instant alternative routes. Driving towards your dream is not so different, but few of us have a handy Dream A–Z at the ready for when we hit obstacles. Having decided on your dream, it makes sense to go through all the possible routes in your mind so that you have given yourself alternative positive choices rather than feeling like a less attractive route has been imposed upon you.

Trick 3: Acknowledge the temporary cause

When you feel utterly miserable and depressed about a setback, it's probably because you think the cause of the problem is permanent. You think you can't change it no matter how hard you try. But look closer: were you tired or run-down that week? Was your head full of other stuff so you didn't really have the time to give your project your full consideration? Looking for realistic but temporary causes helps you bounce back from adversities that may have floored you before. The truth is, rarely is a setback a permanent obstacle to being number one in your own world.

Trick 4: Choose an inspiring mantra for low or panic times
A woman I know repeats a saying every time a challenge comes her way – in fact, she has it pinned on her study wall. It's a famous saying by philosopher, Friedrich Nietzsche, which goes 'That which does not kill us, makes us stronger'. What I particularly like about this saying (and I've said it to myself in all sorts of situations from the trivial to the disastrous) is that it instantly puts obstacles into perspective. And the added bonus is that it's incredibly empowering. Once repeated, it's amazing how quickly you feel able to dust yourself down and move on from disappointment, however severe. Use this saying if you like, or find one that works for you.

Trick 5: Let obstacles help – not hinder – you
Rarely does an obstacle hurtle itself in your way that you cannot learn something from – about yourself, about other people, or about society. The obstacle may have caused

you anything from inconvenience to dreadful pain, but the only way to avoid it in the future is to learn from the experience. When I asked novelist Ruth Rendell how she dealt with hindrances, she said 'Experience is a very good teacher, but charges high wages'. True, isn't it? The point is not to allow those high wages to bankrupt you, but to get value for money from the teachings of experience.

Trick 6: Identify responsibility

Women are particularly prone to feeling responsible, even guilty, for everything that happens not only to them, but to the world as well. For instance, you organize a grand garden party and it rains. Chances are, most of us would bore our guests with apologies for the bad weather. Mad, isn't it? Now I'm not saying we should always blame others and shun responsibility for obstacles in our path to that coveted number one slot. Not at all. But taking all the responsibility all the time is debilitating and confidence crushing. I laughed when chiropodist Deborah Warwick-Jones told me how she jumps over hurdles in her path: 'By sticking up two fingers along the way and moving on,' she said. 'For instance, if I don't get a job, I'll tell myself they didn't really know what they wanted.' This kind of acknowledgement that the obstacle was as a result not of lacking skills, but not having the skills someone else was searching for, is healthy. Going on to equip yourself with both sets of skills, however, is healthier still. It will enable you to jump this hurdle easily and, who knows, remove any hurdles in the future.

Trick 7: Shred the setback

Literally. Write down the obstacle that got in your way, whether it was allowing yourself to be bullied by a relative or your boss, or not getting the promotion you felt you deserved, or being turned down by your bank manager for the loan that would have got your small business idea off the ground. Whatever it is, write it on a piece of paper, take a deep breath, exhale and then rip it to shreds. There! In doing so, tell yourself that this obstacle has gone and is forgotten from here on in. This will help you move forward in your dream positively.

Trick 8: Remember the hurdles you've already jumped

When we hit a hurdle, it's so easy to allow ourselves to be consumed by the challenge. But focusing on the problems that face us in pursuit of our dream without acknowledging the triumphs we've already notched up is to deny ourselves the ego-boost we need at times like this. Janice Graham, a Professor at The Royal College of Music and Leader of the English Symphonia and BBC National Orchestra of Wales, remembers what she calls one of her 'biggest setbacks':

When I started with the London Symphony Orchestra as Principal 2nd Violin, it took a long time for me to get the step up to Assistant Leader. And at one point, I was actually rejected which was difficult for me to handle because I really felt I could do the job. It happened while we were on tour in Japan and I had months of feeling bad about it. The way I got over it was by reminding myself that so much had gone right for me that something else would — and it did.

That's the point, isn't it? The challenges we've overcome never seem so great as the ones we face. But remember that, at the time, they were just as intimidating and success-threatening. That you overcame them and triumphed means you can again ... and again ... and again.

CHAPTER 11

Staying at Number One

Hurrah! You got here! You had a dream — whatever that dream may have been, however big or small — and you made it to where you wanted to be. How do you feel? Elated? Sure you do. Proud of yourself? Of course — and so you should. You have been courageous, determined, kind to others and yourself, focused, crazy (some would say insane, but what the hell?), cheeky, smart, confident, the best you can be. You feel delighted that your life has had a purpose — happiness and fulfilment — and that this purpose has been fulfilled? Fabulous! You truly deserve congratulation of the highest order. No two ways about it — you have succeeded. It may not be success on anyone else's terms, but you don't give a flying fig about anyone else's terms. This is your life and you have made it what you wanted it to be, and that is the success that truly counts and has real meaning. You followed your star and you are a star. Wow! Have a bottle of champagne — no, have ten! Take a lap of honour, take two. Who cares that everyone wants to go home, take a hundred! Enjoy your curtain call, soak up the applause of others, yes, but more importantly, listen to and enjoy your own internal applause, because you *deserve* it.

No one can take credit for you being number one in your own world as much as you, because you did it. Very, very, very, very, *very* well done.

So what now? Having achieved number one status in your own world, you'll sure as hell want to hang on to it – already you'll know being number one in your own world is way, way better than not doing your best, not being at the top of your game. But does achieving goals mean you can stop striving? Indeed, is there any such thing as being number one with knobs on?

Everyone with whom I've talked this through agrees that becoming number one in your own world is wonderful, but it requires work and endurance to maintain that position – whether it's in your relationships, your hobby or your chosen career. It may have been a real challenge to give yourself permission to dream about being number one in your own world in the first place. And often the struggle of making your dream come true can seem just too tough (as we know now, in-flight turbulence is invariably the most uncomfortable aspect of a difficult and complicated journey). But staying at number one can be even tougher. In many cases, it's this knowledge that can stop many people not only from pursuing their dreams, but from dreaming in the first place.

Behavioural habits and attitudes can be learned – and I hope you've learned some great ones from this book – but they can also be forgotten. What's more, new skills are required to enhance the longevity of what you have. After all, having struggled with your sense of self as well as your circumstances and events along the way, do you really want to throw it all away? Many would like to see you do this. After all, it will make them feel better about their own lives and the dreams they never realized. But do you want to give them the satisfaction? More importantly, do you want to return to the emptiness you may have felt before you started following the advice in this book? Of course not.

Arriving at that most coveted position of number one in your own world does not necessarily mean the only way for you to go now is down. Others may enjoy reminding you of this possibility, and yes, the possibility can become a reality – if you allow it. But remember, you are in control. You were the one who got you there and you are the one who can keep you there.

Enjoy being number one in your own world. Now, ensure it lasts for the rest of your life ...

Keep Your Eye on the Number One Slot

When Zsa Zsa Gabor said 'Husbands are like fire; they go out if unattended', she could well have also been talking about being number one in your own world. Because dreams, once achieved, aren't guaranteed forever. They need maintenance. They need feeding.

Arriving where you want to be is a delicious feeling. The sense of accomplishment is empowering and life-affirming. At last, with a true sense of self and purpose, you feel at ease and comfortable with your surroundings and excited by your future. Wonderful! But allowing that comfort to turn into complacency is dangerous; what's also dangerous is that it can happen unintentionally. You simply took your eye off the number one slot.

So what does this mean? On a personal level, you may have allowed the day-to-day desires of others to take precedent over your own. You may have done this once or twice – after all, we shouldn't forget that compromise is a necessary requirement of healthy, mature, loving relation-ships. But when once or twice becomes six or seven times, a pattern of behaviour begins to unfold that can spiral out of your control. Power struggles within relationships are normal, of course. But most relationships that founder do so due to the misery of one half when they feel utterly powerless; when they feel their needs and desires are not being met (at least half of the time), that they are no longer number one in their world, but way down at the bottom of the food chain.

On a professional level, you may have been focused on your dreams and objectives to enable you to get where you wanted to be, but once you've arrived, the focus you had begins to wane. Oh, you still want to be great, whether as an employee or an employer, it's just that, well, the competition is tough which makes you doubt your abilities, and you hit an obstacle which chips away at your self-esteem. Or – and this can be worse – having achieved such an enormous goal, you no longer feel you need to stretch yourself, take risks, grab opportunities. Before you know it, those you work with (other colleagues) or against (competing departments or businesses) are milking the opportunities instead, storming ahead and flourishing, and suddenly – whoops! – you are no longer in control of what or where you want to be. You are a pawn to be moved by others, no longer in control of your destiny.

So how do you keep focused on being number one in your own world once you have arrived? How do you ensure that, either on a personal or professional level, the only way isn't down? Answer: treat your life like a business, because if you don't keep a sharp eye on your investment (your sense of self), it'll go bust. Just imagine if the board of directors of MyLife plc said 'Oh leave the firm to look after itself. As long as we're here, it'll be alright'. The business world would consider them not only dangerously neglectful, but a little crazy, too. And damned right.

Every year, companies get the accountants in to examine the books. They scrutinize what's in credit, what's not, what's worth investing in and what's worth letting go. Bad habits – such as allowing others to take you for granted, doubting your judgement – eat away at your capital. A regular life audit could redeem those draining elements

and stave off self-esteem bankruptcy and ensure you remain
number one in your own world. Don't wait until you've lost
your prized slot. Ask yourself regularly: is my business
(me) where it should be? Do my life books balance up?

How to Keep Your Life Ledger in the Black

- *Take a quick survey of the general wellbeing of your life*
  Is your life becoming stuck in a rut? Is it changing —
  improving or heading downhill? Are there any issues
  eating away at your happiness? Olympic swimmer and
  television presenter, Sharron Davies, told me:

> *Getting the job as presenter of* The Big Breakfast *was really
> exciting. I thought, this is it. I've made it. This is what I want to
> do. But what was offered was not what it ended up being. It
> began to kill me, getting up at 3am, and the show was chang-
> ing, getting younger, and I didn't feel right about doing it. In
> the end, the cost wasn't worth what I was getting from it. But
> I learned from the experience; most importantly, I learned what I
> didn't* want to do.

Sharron's life audit instantly made her realize she wasn't
being number one in her world. What the producers
of *The Big Breakfast* wanted was overtaking her needs,
and it was making her miserable. Sure, everyone else
was impressed by her early-morning TV success, but
this kind of success wasn't success in her eyes. It was

compromise, ignoring her instincts, not fulfilling what Sharron believed was her own potential.

■ *Ask yourself the following questions*
  1 Am I getting from my life what I want?
  2 What am I getting from my life that I don't want?
  3 What am I giving that I don't want to give?
  4 How can I get my attitudes and behaviour back on track so I'm number one in my own world?

A recent *Cosmo* case study interested me. It focused on Lorna who, when she met Steve, was strong, motivated and independent. Their relationship flourished because they shared equal power – much as Lorna adored being with Steve, she maintained her own sense of space and self. She was number one in her world and Steve was number one in his, which resulted in a respectful and exciting relationship. Lorna and Steve went from brilliant to even better, so that within a very short space of time, they decided to live together. But what happened? Lorna said:

I was so excited to be living with Steve, but he moved in and all his stuff was still in boxes six months later – apart from what he'd pulled out and strewn all over the floor. It was driving me nuts.

Lorna felt herself slipping from number one in her own world to number two as she bottled up her anger and frustration at Steve's lack of respect for the flat she'd worked so hard to pull together. She felt taken for granted. Lorna also felt she was compromising her own living standards – her natural behaviour was tidy and particular but she was allowing herself to live according to Steve's scattier lifestyle. Finally, Lorna became so miserable that her once perfect relationship as well as perfect flat had slid into compromise and squalor that, she remembers, 'we had a blow-up'. It wasn't the end of the relationship, thankfully, because prompted by friends, Lorna and Steve gave their life an audit:

Steve was willing to pay half for a cleaner, but not to do half of the cleaning. So now we've a cleaner. And we agreed he'd do the shopping and handle the household finances if I tidied and cooked. And we'd both wash up. Now we're back to being happy again. Thank God.

What's more, Lorna was back to being number one in her world and Steve was back to being number one in his. They had each compromised, yes, but they were able to co-exist according to rules they were both (rather than just one of them) happy with.

■ *Re-establish your hopes, wishes and dreams*

Remember the dream plan you made before you reached where you wanted to be? Revisit it regularly. How does the reality of the life you're living right now compare? Do you still feel exhilarated, valued, excited about your future? Are your instinct antennae as finely-tuned as they were or are they beginning to fuzz from probing the vibes from other people? If you haven't yet achieved your big dream, are you still on course? If you have achieved your dream, consider what you want from your next step and where you want to head in the future. How you deal with the wellbeing of your hopes, wishes and dreams now determines whether MyLife plc continues to boom well into the millennium.

> In my job I review clients' businesses three times a year: reviewing objectives and examining whether those objectives have been met. It's essential you do the same with your life. Take stock and ask yourself 'Am I where I want to be?'. It keeps you motivated and focused on what you want.
>
> **Jenny Swift, Director, Ketchum Life PR agency**

Do Your Best

I remember vividly when I became Editor of *Cosmopolitan*. It was the result of years of hard work, it was my dream realized. Forty-eight hours after my appointment, I slumped. I felt unspeakably miserable, desolate even. I couldn't fathom it. What was my problem? Thankfully, I had a patient, willing-to-listen husband and an ever-supportive mother who coaxed out of me my true feelings about my arrival at my dream. It can be summed up in four crucial letters. F.E.A.R. Oh no, the dreaded word. Fear that having achieved my ultimate career dream I would let everyone down, including myself. Fear that I wasn't bright enough to edit this amazing magazine. Fear that I wasn't stylish enough to represent the glamour of the *Cosmopolitan* woman. Fear, fear, fear. After hours of convincing, I remember clear as the day, my mother stating in semi-exasperation, 'Mandi, you can only do your best. You've done your best all your life and you've been great. Just do your best. The only way you will let anyone down, including you, is if you don't do your best.'

That was one of the best pieces of advice I have ever been given, and let me tell you, in subsequent moments of fear, I have repeated it to myself with empowering effect. Because if nothing else is within your control, doing your best is. Getting to number one requires doing – and feeling – your best at everything; staying at number one requires even more of your best. In my case, staying at number one requires that I not only do my best, but that I inspire others to do their best, too. Which is why, before I see any copy or pictures or listen to ideas, I ask each one of my staff to ask themselves 'Is this the very best I can do?'. If they can't sincerely answer yes, then I ask that they don't even present it to me. What's more, when others know you're doing the best you possibly can, it inspires them to match your effort. It's the ultimate benchmark of excellence.

Fending off the Competition

Doing your very best not only means you are automatically fulfilling your potential in whatever you're doing, it also means you are stretching yourself, giving that extra little push when you almost feel you can't exert yourself any further, which invariably puts you ahead of the rest.

It's exhausting, yes, but it's energizing, too. On a professional level, those who are number one in their own world never settle for good enough. They know if they do, there will be someone else right alongside them giving that little bit extra – and taking over that number one slot. Instead they ask themselves, 'Is this the very best I can do?'. They never allow themselves to become complacent, and never believe in the lasting power of past achievements. It's the excellence of what you do in the present that keeps you in the number one slot.

Janice Graham who is, among other credits to her name, Leader of the BBC National Orchestra of Wales and Assistant Leader of the London Symphony Orchestra, says this:

I have achieved much more than I thought I would have by this age. It's partly talent, but it's also about application, doing your very best at all times. But I never lose the wish to get better. While at 30, I am the number one orchestral leader in Cardiff, I know you're only ever as good as your last concert. But what motivates me is the desire to improve, do even better. I am motivated by perfection. If I were to give any advice for being number one in your own world? Always, always do your best.

You can apply the same philosophy to your relationships, too. Do your best for friends, lovers and family and they will generally do their best for you. One of the first signs that a relationship will hit the rocks is when one or both parties stops trying or only inputs mediocre effort. Think about the couples you've seen in restaurants slurping their supper in silence, never once making the effort to chat, enquire, show interest. Should it surprise anyone that an affair begins with another partner who plans exciting or different things to do, who dresses up, asks interested questions and listens to the answers, isn't so smug or complacent about the relationship that they become dull, irritating, pompous, unattractive?

Doing Your Best for Now – and Your Future

Just because you've attained the number one slot, it doesn't mean that this glory is all there is. If it were, what a shallow, pointless struggle to the top it would be. No, success is like a river that needs to keep flowing. If it stops, it can easily turn into a stagnant pool. Being number one with knobs on means paving the way for future, even bigger, successes. It's about impressing others who can present you with new, stimulating opportunities; it's about preventing boredom, keeping inspired and energized, and opening yourself up to new exciting avenues. As Oprah Winfrey once said, 'Doing the best at this moment puts you in the best place for the next moment'.

Take Pride in Your Achievements

Getting to number one in your own world is one of the greatest achievements anyone could boast of. The courage, determination and strength of character it requires to live according to your own rules and succeed on your own terms within your own parameters is something of which you have the right to be inordinately proud. Being focused on your achievements and using them to inspire and moti- vate you into pursuing your dreams even further – or at the very least, maintaining your dreams – is crucial.

Certainly in the British culture, we're taught from a very young age to be modest about our achievements. It's regarded as distasteful behaviour to congratulate your- self on your accomplishments. Self-deprecation – putting yourself and your achievements down – is a quality the British in particular admire and applaud. Self-pride, on the other hand, is regarded as conceited, vulgar and arro- gant. Good grief! It's a wonder anyone dares to have a dream, never mind – God forbid – achieve anything of merit.

Keeping your feet on the ground is great in some respects, but I can think of very few. In interviews with successful people, modesty is often presented as admirable, but maybe that's because it makes the interviewer feel better about their lack of aspiration. Okay, if pushed, I'll concede that a feet-on-the-ground approach means you're not so high and mighty that you stop listening to others' opinions and therefore stop learning (and we'll come on to the importance of this a bit further on). But keeping your feet on the ground too much can inhibit your view of risk and opportunity and prevent you enjoying the rewards you deserve for your success.

Just because you've become number one in your own world doesn't mean blips in self-confidence will never strike again. And if you don't allow yourself to recap on your achievements and take pride in them, those natural insecurities we all have can rise up and overshadow our ability to maintain our success. I've already confessed to you the feelings of fear I experienced when I landed my dream job, Editor of *Cosmopolitan*. Now let me tell you something else I experienced at that time: finding myself thrust into the public eye, I was astonished by the battering I received from other journalists. It was extremely painful and humiliating (journalists are super-critical of other journalists).

At the time when I most needed my confidence and self-belief, attempts to erode it were occurring on a daily basis. In fact, the question 'Who the hell does she think she is?' was asked so often, I started to ask myself the same thing. Eventually, after a couple of weeks of upset over inconsequential, often envy-driven, subjective baloney, I arrived at the answer: the best person for the job actually. Which is why I got the job, of course – and they didn't. But I only arrived at this (logical) conclusion after a great deal of, let's call it, 'achievement analysis'. Recapping on past triumphs, congratulating myself on achievements from the biggest to the smallest boosted my self-esteem and reinforced the self-belief that wasn't just instrumental in getting me to number one (in my own world) but is critical to keeping me there. Nothing written about me since has had such an effect. Not because what's been written hasn't been as bitter and insulting (because it has), but because I am fantastically proud of my achievements and truly believe, even if no one else does, that they deserve such pride.

The truth is, when you are number one in your own world, there will inevitably be those who undermine your achievements. Maybe they won't see them as achievements at all. After all, what is an incredible achievement to you can be daily routine to another. Maybe they see your achievement as a threat to their own journey. Maybe your achievements cause them to face up to their own ... or lack of them. But however others respond to you and how you've chosen to live your life, it should not erode your own personal sense of pride.

While I'm at it, attempting to make others feel better by dismissing what you have achieved is to be avoided at all costs. What good is there in doing that? I've tried it a couple of times and it made me despise that person as well as myself. If they're a friend and you have to behave like this around them, maybe it's time to reconsider the value of your friendship, rather than the value of your achievement. If they're an employee, isn't it better to inspire them to achieve by your own example rather than allow them to believe that achievements are worthless? If they're an employer, tell yourself you should be going for their job (if that's what you want) and go for it or take your skills where they will be appreciated, your achievements encouraged and your potential allowed to flourish even further. If they're a lover or spouse, I hesitate to say this, but … have you thought of finding yourself another who will enjoy basking in your reflected glory and appreciate you for what you are: number one in your own world? And absolutely, undeniably, you-niquely *great!*

> *Don't be embarrassed by your achievements. Being an over-achiever is nothing despicable. It is only admirable. Never lower your standards.*
>
> **Martha Stewart, businesswoman**

Know Your Achievement is Real (So Don't Feel Like a Fake)

When you get to number one in your own world – land the job you wanted, establish the position you're happy with in your relationship, win a recording contract, set up the tea shop you've always dreamed you'd own, whatever – acknowledging that you arrived here by your sheer power, skill, determination and courage is fantastically important if you're to stay here. Yes, you may have taken a little help from other people when offered; okay, some circumstances or breaks may have been fortunate or paid off (note, I didn't say lucky); but however you arrived, it was you and only you who had the dream, bought the book, laid plans, put them into action, nourished and stuck with them and got you there.

What I'm getting at is the tendency, certainly among women, to feel like a fake. In other words, they feel they don't deserve their success, that achieving it must have been a sheer fluke because they don't feel smart or witty or stylish enough to warrant such achievement. You recognize the syndrome?

This feeling can easily creep up on anyone, especially if they aren't used to having aspirations and achieving them. If success in any area of our life feels alien to us ("Success is what happens to others, not me"), then when we experience the delicious taste of it, we feel so wonderful we start to worry. We not only worry it will be taken away from us at any moment, but we also worry that somehow it's all been a happy coincidence "something this great can't possibly have been made by me!"

When people congratulate us, we can feel like a fraudster for accepting praise – after all, praise is only deserved after genuine back-breaking achievement. We not only think but can actually believe "As I'm not really smart or quick or stylish or whatever enough to have achieved this great dream, it must have been luck. Therefore, praise isn't warranted." Etc. etc. etc.

You may have used up so much of your newly acquired self-confidence reserves that, once you have achieved your dream, you don't recognize the person who got you there. You feel overwhelmed by your achievements, full of self-doubt ("can I really be so great?"), unable now to match how others see your ability and competence with how you see them. You feel unable to live up to your dream. I know this is how many people feel because we received such a huge response to a feature on the subject when we tackled it in *Cosmopolitan*. So many women identified with the undeniably successful, Oscar-winning actress Emma Thompson who confessed she still felt like an ugly failure, despite the accolades and golden gongs. We called this feeling 'Achilles Syndrome' after the mythical Greek warrior who was thought to be invincible, but had a vulnerable place on his heel that led to his death.

One woman, Jayne, told us how her feelings nearly destroyed her. At 27, she had achieved her dream – she was a big shot in the City, a project financier who was considered one of the best workers on her team, and had a wonderful relationship with a man who both respected and encouraged her. In short, she was number one in her own world:

I was considered the real golden girl at work. At appraisals, managers would always say the same things — I was thoroughly competent, an asset. But it felt as if they were talking about someone else. The higher I climbed, the worse it became as I felt more of a fake and had more to lose by admitting it. Eventually, I resigned before they realized I couldn't really do the job at all.

For the next year, Jayne was unemployed. What's more, she split with the boyfriend she adored under the strain:

It seems irrational now. When I quit they couldn't believe it. But even then, I thought they were just being polite. They were thinking of sending me to New York to head up a project — but that just petrified me even more, so I left.

It took Jayne over six months to rebuild the confidence that had taken her to the top in the first place, but only after being on the brink of a breakdown which forced her to share her true feelings with a friend. And guess what? Jayne's friend confessed she too sometimes felt this way, as did most people she knew:

Once I had no reason left to pretend — because no one was saying how fantastic I was anymore — I could admit how I felt. It was a revelation. Whenever I'd expressed self-doubt before, everyone said it was false modesty. Or they said 'You've managed brilliantly before, you'll be fine this time'. But it was because I found it diffi-cult to draw any confidence from previous success that I'd quit under the strain of it all.

Jayne is now back at work as a leader of a team of 10 and feels so much better equipped to deal with each new chal-lenge. She has learned confidence tricks to boost her self-esteem when it flags. What's more, she's realized that just because you are number one, it doesn't mean you can't continue to ask for help when you need it. It was a painful lesson for Jayne, but having come through to the other side, she says, 'The best thing is now I can actually enjoy my success.'

Before Achilles Syndrome gets the better of you:

- Come clean to a trusted friend or lover about how you feel. Knowing that others often feel the same puts your negative feelings back into perspective.
- Remind yourself that even if you fake confidence it doesn't make it less valid. Acting confident is 50 per cent of being confident. Acting knowledgeable is halfway to achieving knowledge.
- Never be afraid to ask for help. Everyone who has ever achieved success in any area of their life has done so

with a little bit of help. It isn't a sign of weakness; it's a sign of strength that you know how to use resources.

- Don't dismiss the methods you have used to achieve your success. Some people achieve success through sheer wit and cheek. Others by intelligence. Often success is achieved through single-minded determination and courage. Invariably, it's as a result of a combination of many actions and unique characteristics. Bottom line: your success is unique because you achieved it your way; it's meaningful and a credit to you however you achieved it.

Keep Learning and Keep Ahead

Those who are number one in their worlds share many glorious characteristics — and I've covered many of them throughout this book — but one of the most significant traits of the truly successful is their on-going desire to learn. They watch, they read, they ask questions, and they listen carefully to the answers. Although they have masses of self-confidence (or at least they've learned the trick of appearing like they do), their egos are not so inflated they believe they know it all. Those who have achieved number one status and stay there have an infinite curiosity and a sponge-like capacity for new information, knowing that every scrap of fresh knowledge is ammunition to keep them ahead.

Whichever world it is in which you desire to be number one, remember it's part of a moving universe. We rarely exist to the exclusion of everything else. Even those who take themselves off to the remotest parts of the globe to pursue their dream are to some extent at the mercy of changing climates and politics. Not acquiring information about those changes is naive and dangerous.

If your world is confined to being number one in your relationship, there is no guarantee that the person with whom you have that relationship will not change, even imperceptibly. No relationship is ever identical 10 years on to how it was at the beginning. Those who truly achieve relationship nirvana are those who never become complacent. They have an insatiable curiosity about themselves and their relationship. They never tire of asking their partner questions, listening to their responses and taking action when required. Let's not forget also the importance of learning about ourselves within that relationship: am I happy? If I'm not happy, why not? Is the relationship I have today with this person the relationship I want tomorrow? If not, what action can I take?

If your dream was to be a number one parent, you cannot be number one in that world if you don't recognize that change happens almost daily and that the child who adored lasagne one moment will loathe it the next. Learning about what makes your growing children tick — asking them why they feel how they feel, acquiring new information about their lives and trying your damnedest to put it to practical use – is essential to maintaining your happiness as well as theirs.

And in business, too, acquiring new skills, learning fresh information about the marketplace, the needs of customers and opinions of those who work with you is key to being number one. You can't assume a product or service will continue to meet demands without learning about changing expectations and requirements. The most successful people in business are constantly on the lookout for new markets, asking their customers and clients how they can improve their service. They use each day as a learning process: why was this successful, why did that not meet our expectations, how can we offer more or better, what's new?

Jennifer Tanfield, Head Librarian at the House of Commons, says, 'I try to do as much listening and as little talking as possible. I try to learn something every day'. Rose Johnson, Chief Inspector of Brent Schools, shares this philosophy, saying, 'Never stop trying to learn. I love learning, even now. I love finding out about people – they never cease to fascinate me. It's one of the best ways to get others to contribute powerfully to the vision you want to make a reality'. And when asked the key to her on-going success, designer Vivienne Westwood replied, 'I always remind myself to question things'.

How to Keep Open to Learning

■ Read as much as you can. You've made a great start buying this book. Flip back and forth when you need to reacquaint yourself with confidence techniques. Buy autobiographies of people you admire – it will not only reinforce the idea that success is available to anyone who wants it, but you'll learn from their experiences, too. Whatever your world is, someone will have written a book on the subject to help you be and stay number one in it.

■ Surround yourself not only with people who share your vision of being number one, but also those who challenge it. Janette Anderson, Director of Railtrack, Scotland, believes it's wise to hire a 'No-man' in business. This isn't someone who's negative (no, no, you don't need that), but someone who has the confidence to challenge you. 'You're not right all of the time,' says Janette. 'A No-man will either offer a different perspective from which you can learn or, in the process of the challenge, convince you further that your opinion is right.'

■ Don't assume you can only learn from those with experience. Entrepreneur Chey Garland makes a point of talking to new recruits to hear their views and suggestions about the work they do, particularly those who are new to the industry. 'I am excited by young people,' she says. 'Even though their ability is raw, they see through different eyes. Experience hasn't dampened their imagination, they bring a fresh perspective that it's impossible to have once entrenched in the industry.' As far as my own career is concerned, I've learned some wonderful things from interviewing people for very junior jobs. I remember one interviewee criticizing a section in the magazine, which, as it happened, I'd been concerned about for some time. It wasn't easy for me to take, but, wow, did I learn big time where I'd been going wrong. Hey presto! A new and improved section in the magazine which scored highly in research among our readers.

■ Don't dismiss the value of your own experiences – learn by them all, however small. You are the best teacher you have. Don't stop learning from your best resource – you.

> *I believe people are in our lives for a reason. We're here to learn from one another.*
>
> **Gillian Anderson, actress**

Keep Setting Yourself Goals – and Achieve Them

> *Physical beauty is ephemeral, but the self-confidence one builds from achieving difficult things and accomplishing goals is the most beautiful thing of all.*
>
> **Madonna**

We know that being number one in your own world means being thrilled and proud of where you are right now, but being and staying number one is a dynamic process which requires stimulation to ensure you're still maximizing your potential.

Once you stop setting yourself goals, you stop growing, you stop reaching your full potential. Would Madonna be the icon she is today if she'd stopped at her first number one hit? No way. Would you admire Gwyneth Paltrow as much if she'd rested on the laurels of her first major film role? I doubt it. Would Tony Blair really have been number one in his own world had he just been content to settle for his first parliamentary seat? Absolutely not, and it's fair to say the world, our world, would have been a very different place for it, too. Those who make a real impact on our world, as well as their own, know that setting goals, grasping even bigger opportunities and achieving even more is crucial to maximizing their potential and being the best they can be.

Now you've arrived at number one in your own world, you have proven you can achieve tons. So what's to say you can't achieve even more? You may wonder what the point is. After all, why not just enjoy what you have? Oh sure, I'm a big advocate of enjoying what you have. But you need to nourish the confidence you've acquired on your journey to number one which allows you to enjoy it, otherwise it can falter. And the novelty of where you are now can lose its sheen if it isn't replenished with new and different experiences. What's more, if your world is a competitive one – say in media, or sport, or sales, or technology – there will inevitably be others nipping at your heels, desperate to take your number one slot should you stop stretching your capabilities and maximizing your full potential.

Nothing beats the high you experience from setting a goal which seems just beyond reach, and then achieving it. Look at the faces of marathon runners when they complete their course. Do they ever look despondent? Ha! Their eyes are shining, their faces, while taut under the strain, are beaming. They may be exhausted, but they're super-energized, massively invigorated. Although this may not be the first time they have run a marathon, the fact that they have completed this one, and maybe in a faster time than the previous attempt, gives them a far bigger boost and confidence injection than simply the knowledge and comfort that they did it once.

Amanda Levete, who is a partner of Future Systems architects, advises against wallowing in the comfort zone of present success:

Don't ever feel too comfortable. Make the most of what you have to offer by pushing yourself constantly to the limit. It can take years to build up a sense of self-confidence, but only five minutes to have it knocked out.

That's so true. I've been on the receiving end of having my self-confidence knocked out, and you know what? It's often been after I've allowed myself to cruise in the comfort zone for a short while. Perhaps I've seen another magazine's cover or read an article I would have killed for in *Cosmo*. Momentarily, my confidence takes a dip and I feel vulnerable and shaky. I could give in to it. I could, but I know that in doing so, I would jeopardize everything I've achieved to date. Instead, I set myself goals. I pick up the telephone and aim to get an even better cover than the one that (almost) sent my confidence levels spiralling downwards. Or I'll make contact with a star writer who previously may have overawed me and ask them to write a brilliant feature exclusively for *Cosmo*. Probably I'll do both, on the basis that even if I achieve only half of my goals, I'll be better placed than I was before. Invariably, both goals are achieved. And *voilà*! A surge of confidence. My self-esteem is restored, I feel proud of myself and, an added bonus, the magazine looks even better.

I've learned the value of this procedure over time. It's one I know works, guaranteed. If I were super-smart, I wouldn't allow myself to set foot in the comfort zone in the first place. I would, unprompted by confidence dips, keep setting goals – and achieve them. But here's my pledge: I will from now on. Will you?

Have Fun and Enjoy Being Number One

When Richard Branson was considering expanding his already successful venture into commercial air travel, his partners thought he'd gone mad. He remembers of that time:

Simon and Ken remained resolutely opposed. 'Come on,' I ploughed on. 'Virgin can afford to make this step. The risk is less than a third of this year's profits ... And it'll be fun.' Simon and Ken both winced when I said 'fun', which is a particularly loaded word for me — it's one of my main business criteria.

Why does it seem incongruous to talk about power, success and fun all in the same breath? Why should success and fun be mutually exclusive? Perhaps because we have been so used to equating success with how much pleasure we sacrifice along the way — remember that miserable old cliché, 'no gain without pain'? Perhaps it's because the word fun is regarded as frivolous, weak and childish, and success is only for the strong, the mature, the logical, to be taken seriously. Seriously successful? Who wants such a thing today? Happily successful? Merrily successful? Joyfully successful? Now *that's* more like true success.

Perhaps the words fun and success appear to be a strange combination because we are only *now* waking up to our new sense of self, the purpose to our lives we discussed back in Chapter 2 which defines success in direct proportion to how happy you feel. Success and being number one in your own world are all about having fun and experiencing the kind of happiness that makes you want to burst with laughter and joy.

Make Fun Your Key Motivator

If fun is the journey as well as the destination, it's also the fuel that enables you to get there, lubricating your motivation and helping to make the journey as obstacle-free as possible. And once you've arrived at destination Dream, fun is also what stops rust setting in, maintains bright lights and keeps your engines roaring. When the fun-brakes go on, it's a sure sign the journey has ceased to be right for you and it's time to reconsider your destination.

Think about all the rewards you can reap from achieving your dreams: money maybe, column inches in the papers perhaps, medals or certificates, love, a big house in the country or a fabulous car, the knowledge that you have helped others realize their dreams ... all these things and more are very nice rewards. But money can also bring with it stress, and column inches in today's paper will, as the saying goes, be tomorrow's fish-and-chip wrappings. Medals and certificates, of course, are great to look at, but collect dust and are so easily lost and forgotten. And the novelty of a bigger house or car soon wears off. The knowledge that you've helped other people realize their dreams is wonderful for making you feel warm and mushy inside. But the truth is, without the experience of fun along the way, these rewards taste ever so slightly sour long-term. They are virtually meaningless with today's sense of self, if fun isn't part of the success cocktail.

I cannot envisage doing the job I do (albeit my dream job) if fun wasn't part of my daily experience. The competitive aspect of my position would have burned me out a long time ago were there no huge guffaws of laughter during ideas meetings to re-energize my batteries and release some of the tension that's part and parcel of a job like this. Keeping within budgets and landing sponsorship deals wouldn't taste half so good (not to mention be practically impossible to achieve in the first place) if part of my week wasn't spent in the fashion cupboard giggling over the latest outrageous outfit or in my office joking with the team or deciding to run a story simply because it would be a hoot, for us as well as the readers. I used to believe my primary motivation for working was money ... until I found myself in a job that paid well, yes, but offered little fun. No amount of money could compensate for feeling ill with misery each weekend at the thought of going back to work on Monday.

I have experienced workplaces where fun is positively frowned upon. The sound of laughter is taken as a sign of time wasting and lack of commitment. My philosophy is quite the opposite. Fun is a sign of time being put to productive use and a very clear indicator of commitment and passion as well as enjoyment.

Sylvia, 42, a neighbour of mine, told me about her experience when I described this final chapter:

From the moment I left university, I wanted to work in marketing. I couldn't imagine anything more fun than understanding people and products and bringing the two together. I worked long and hard, rose through the ranks quickly and, by my mid-30s, was the deputy managing director of a leading marketing company. 'Fabulous,' I thought, 'I'm where I wanted to be in my career, and I can afford the house of my dreams and as many designer clothes as I can get my hands on. But over the next few months, I became so utterly depressed, I couldn't even haul myself out of bed at the weekends to go and shop for the clothes I'd fantasized about. You know what I spent my money on? Massages and beauty treatments to make myself feel better and, sad to say, expensive bottles of wine and spirits … the only time I was able to laugh was when I'd had a drink.

I asked Sylvia why she was so depressed. After all, her dreams, it seemed, had come true. She told me:

Each day, I'd put my favourite tape on as I drove to work to get me in a happy frame of mind. But as soon as I walked into the office, my spirits would plummet. It was so quiet. There was no camaraderie. There were no whoops of joy when we landed new business.

There were no screams of encouragement when we hit difficult periods. There was no laughter. Ever. I tried to change the culture of suspicion, pessimism and misery, but I was a lone voice. In the end, I couldn't take any more unhappiness. I cut my losses — I handed back the car, gave up my expense account, put my wardrobe fantasies on hold and quit.

The day I did that was the happiest day of my life. When you're having fun, you take it for granted. When you're not, you realize it's the most important thing in life. My friends and family thought I was crazy. Only my husband understood — he'd experienced enough of my depression to know I had to do this. It really was a case of do or die. Now I have my own small market research company. It's tough — boy, it's soooo tough — and sometimes I wonder, even though we've moved to a smaller house and traded in our big family car for a Ford Fiesta, how we're going to get through the month. But the fun I have at work with my small team of people who understand that having fun is what it's all about, not only makes me tons happier at work — not to mention better at work — but happier at home, on holiday, and at weekends.

But, I asked Sylvia, doesn't she ever feel regretful that she had to abandon her dream of being a high-flying marketing executive?

You talk of being number one in your own world. How can you be number one in your own world if you're so unhappy you even contemplate ending it all? It isn't your level of earnings that makes you number one in your own world. It's the level of fun you have in your life. I've experienced both and I know the latter is the true definition of being number one in your own world.

Hooray to that!

> *Life is made of time. Use it and enjoy it. It's all you've got.*
> **Claire Rayner**

Fun is for Life – not Just for Work

For most of us, being number one in your own world rarely revolves around work alone. So it's worth mentioning that relationships – whether with friends, relatives or lovers – founder because the fun has disappeared. Yes, sharing common goals and values is important. Yes, having the same attitudes towards religion and money and sex is healthy, too. But what's the one characteristic the majority of lonely hearts request in their search for love? You guessed it: a sense of humour. In other words, someone to have fun with, share jokes with and make them laugh. And it's precisely the lack of this that drives a wedge between even the most compatible couples. When people have fun together, the experience can transcend all manner of cultural and moral differences, which is why it isn't uncommon to see friendships across colours and cultures, relationships that blossom despite age gaps spanning generations, and matches made in heaven between lovers at extreme ends of the 'beauty' spectrum. We hear of communities being united by grief and sadness, but as we know, this can become exhausting and negative. The bond created by happiness, joy and fun is far more long-lasting, as well as positive.

A good friend of mine called Tricia knows all about the importance of fun in relationships. She endured a fun-less marriage for eight years:

I left school and landed a good job almost immediately. Then, shortly afterwards, I met Andy in a bar and within eight months, we were married. My friends couldn't believe it — I had always been the ultimate good-time party girl. But I often felt empty and lonely and Andy seemed so grown-up and wise. I thought he was just what I was looking for to make me feel like a whole person, complete. The first year was dreamy — we ate at expensive restaurants, took sailing holidays, went walking in the country. But slowly, Andy's outlook on the world started to rub off. He was so melancholic, I almost felt guilty for having fun when he wasn't around. I stopped seeing my friends, stopped staying for a drink after work, I even stopped dressing in a way that I felt happy with. Yes, my new style was smart, but it was so ... beige and old. Instead of going out at the weekend, we'd stay in with a video and a takeaway. Rather than go on holiday with friends, we'd just hire a cottage, the two of us, and have early nights. All our friends thought we were the perfect couple — and I guess on paper we were — but I was beginning to think differently ... Our relationship wasn't fun. He wasn't fun. I wasn't fun anymore. The crunch came when we attended a wedding last year. During the service, I couldn't stop crying. Andy was embarrassed as he thought I was being over-emotional. But what I couldn't tell him was that the couple getting married looked so happy, like they were having so much fun, it made me realize all the fun had gone out of our relationship. I couldn't remember a time when Andy and I had actually laughed together.

I tried to talk through the way I felt with Andy. I tried suggesting new, exciting things we could do together as a couple. I got nowhere. Soon, I stopped going home as the atmosphere felt as though it was crushing me, squeezing all the life out of me. Finally, I plucked up the courage to tell Andy our marriage was over. I came to the conclusion that I felt so lonely in our marriage, the loneliness of being single couldn't possibly be worse.

We're divorced now. I'm not proud of myself. I know I hurt Andy a lot. But staying would have hurt him even more. And staying would have killed me. I want to have fun. If life isn't about having fun, what is it about?

Fun – the Final Arbiter

Think about all the experiences in your life you'd want to repeat. An amazing holiday, a shopping trip where you bought a trillion items that made you look and feel wonderful, a dinner party where everyone clicked and roared with laughter between one course and the next, landing a job you never thought you'd get and the way it made you skip down the road, smiling to yourself, making you want to rush up to the nearest person and give them a huge, giddy hug. This is fun. This is what life and being number one in your life is about. This emotion is available to you

How to Be Number One in Your Own World

every day, if only you'd create the opportunities for it to rear up and take a hold on you.

As I write this final chapter about being number one in your own world, I can hear my two daughters upstairs. It's almost eight o'clock and they should be asleep. But instead of silence, I can hear them laughing. Not just stifled giggles, mind you, but roaring, explosive belly laughs. A toy or book has crashed to the floor and Rosie, my eldest, has squealed her high-pitched laugh, while Daisy, my youngest, is laughing so hard and deep it's making me laugh, too. It's the most wonderful sound in the whole wide world and I wish I could bottle it forever.

Should I rush upstairs and tell them to pipe down? Should I remind them they have school tomorrow and they may well be tired if they keep laughing? Should I tell them if they keep making me laugh, preventing me from concentrating, I may not finish this chapter and therefore over-run my deadline even more?

Absolutely not. Their laughter shows they're having fun, that their life is happy. This is what will motivate them tomorrow to pursue their dreams, not fun-crushing discipline. Sure, if it goes on until midnight, I'll take a risk (because risk-taking is good) and tell them to go to sleep (because, as we all now know, being number one in your own world takes effort), but, listen … already I can hear them quietening down of their own accord. No doubt when I go upstairs shortly, they'll be snoring like two little trains, happy they had fun and looking forward to tomorrow when fun, again, is a real possibility.

And anyway, their laughter and my laughter reminds me, as if I should really need it, that this is really what being number one in your own world is all about. It makes the negative experiences I've had yesterday and today fade away — hell, I can hardly even remember what it was that infuriated or disappointed or upset me. Although it's late, and I need to finish this book tonight, their laughter and my laughter are the two elements that are motivating and energizing me. This tiny-in-the-scheme-of-things experience tonight has absolutely reinforced my belief that fun and happiness are the ultimate litmus test of the life you want to lead.

Stand back and take stock of your life with a smile on your face. Yes, there will be day-to-day hitches, glitches and downright hassles. But if you're having fun, that's the biggest reward for being successful, being number one in your own world. Now if you want to stay there forever, for crying out loud, *enjoy* it.

Afterword

I truly hope you have enjoyed this book, that you feel inspired to take on the world and fulfil your dreams. Being number one in your own world is there for the taking, whatever it means to you, so make sure you do take it. Inevitably, there will be times when your tenacity takes a knock, when you may feel that, for the short-term at least, it's easier to let others take control of your life or when the sound of those ridiculing your dreams becomes so loud it drowns out your self-motivation and belief. But remember, if you give in to those doubts, the only loser in your life will be you.

Now you have finished reading this book, don't store it away on your bookshelf. Use it to drip-feed yourself with encouragement and self-belief. Keep it by your bed or on your coffee table. Use highlighter pen to score paragraphs you find particularly inspiring. Or cut them out and stick them on your fridge or pinboard. Dog-ear the corners of pages that contain phrases or mottoes that charge you up. Write your own thoughts and experiences in ink against relevant sections. Why not tear out chapters and carry them with you every day in your bag?

I'd hate to think the effect of this book on your life was temporary, lasting only as long as it took you to read it. After all, the desire and motivation to be number one in your own world is one that requires sustaining all your life. And the actions you're inspired to take today require encouragement tomorrow and the day after ... and the day after that.

There is no state of being better than number one in your own world. You now believe it isn't a privilege, but your right, and what you wholeheartedly deserve.

Now go for it. Be number *one* — and *enjoy!*

Appendix

New Rules for Life
33 Ways to be Number One in Your Own World

1 Forget about decisions you made in the past that didn't work out. Focus on what you can change.

2 Don't give away your power. Don't turn over your life to your friends or your money to a lover. No one should be in charge of your life, except you.

3 Stay away from negative people. It's contagious.

4 Life is not a race to the finish. It's a journey to a prize.

5 Don't be afraid of competition. Look at it as a teaching method.

6 Never just 'settle'.

7 Aim for the sky. Your arrow will fly much higher than if you'd only aimed for eye level.

8 Unplug your people-pleasing machine. So long as you know you're a good egg, yours is the only opinion that matters.

9 Drop out of the comparathon. Obsessing over your have-not status sucks the air out of your self-esteem.

10 You don't *have* to do anything. Slavery was abolished a century ago.

11 Don't even try to be all things to all people. Just be one thing: you.

12 No one can intimidate you. Only your own fears can allow you to feel intimidated.

13 Only do what you want to do, not what you *ought* to do.

14 You're never too young or too old to think big.

15 You only regret the things you don't do.

16 If you behave like a doormat, people will wipe their feet on you.

17 If you aren't number one in your world, you will be number one in no world.

18 Move forward with the current of your own soul.

19 This day will never come again. So do it now.

20 If you want sunshine, you have to be prepared for a few showers.

21 Follow *your* star. There are enough stars in the galaxy of opportunities for everyone.

22 Words = 2. Actions = 10. Dreams don't happen if you simply talk about them.

23 Take a small risk every day and feel your confidence grow.

24 Never feel remorse about breaking rules.

25 Be prepared to sacrifice the small details for the big dream.

26 Don't listen to self-named 'experts' with lists of reasons why your vision has no merit.

27 Dare to be different – it's the catalyst of all great enterprise.
28 Don't focus on where you've come from, but where you're going to.
29 If it feels right to you, it *is* right.
30 Be inspired by change, not inhibited by it.
31 Don't wait for the right day to go after your dreams. Today is the right day.
32 There's nothing wrong with being a thinker. Just make sure you're a doer, too. Thinking gives birth to fantasies. Doing makes fantasies reality.
33 Remember, you're not perfect. You're better than that – you're you-nique!